BY LARRY McMURTRY

The Berrybender Narratives

Hollywood: A Third Memoir

Literary Life: A Second Memoir

Rhino Ranch

Books: A Memoir

When the Light Goes

Telegraph Days

Oh What a Slaughter

The Colonel and Little Missie

Loop Group

Folly and Glory

By Sorrow's River

The Wandering Hill

Sin Killer

Sacagawea's Nickname: Essays on the American West

Paradise

Boone's Lick

Roads

Still Wild: Short Fiction of the American West, 1950 to the Present

Walter Benjamin at the Dairy Queen

Duane's Depressed

Crazy Horse

Comanche Moon

Dead Man's Walk

The Late Child

Streets of Laredo

The Evening Star

Buffalo Girls

Some Can Whistle

Anything for Billy

Film Flam: Essays on Hollywood

Texasville

Lonesome Dove

The Desert Rose

Cadillac Jack

Somebody's Darling

Terms of Endearment

All My Friends Are Going to Be Strangers

Moving On

The Last Picture Show

In a Narrow Grave: Essays on Texas

Leaving Cheyenne

Horseman, Pass By

BY LARRY McMURTRY AND DIANA OSSANA

Pretty Boy Floyd

Zeke and Ned

CUSTER

LARRY McMURTRY

Simon & Schuster Paperbacks

New York   London   Toronto   Sydney   New Delhi

Simon & Schuster Paperbacks
A Division of Simon & Schuster, Inc.
1230 Avenue of the Americas
New York, NY 10020

Copyright © 2012 by Larry McMurtry

All rights reserved, including the right to reproduce this book or
portions thereof in any form whatsoever. For information address
Simon & Schuster Paperback Subsidiary Rights Department,
1230 Avenue of the Americas, New York, NY 10020

First Simon & Schuster paperback edition October 2013

SIMON & SCHUSTER PAPERBACKS and colophon are registered
trademarks of Simon & Schuster, Inc.

For information about special discounts for bulk purchases,
please contact Simon & Schuster Special Sales at
1-866-506-1949 or business@simonandschuster.com.

The Simon & Schuster Speakers Bureau can bring authors
to your live event. For more information or to book an event,
contact the Simon & Schuster Speakers Bureau at
1-866-248-3049 or visit our website at www.simonspeakers.com.

Designed by Nancy Singer

Photography and Art Consultant: Kevin Kwan

Manufactured in the United States of America

3   5   7   9   10   8   6   4   2

The Library of Congress has cataloged the hardcover as follows

McMurty, Larry.
Custer/Larry McMurtry.
pages   cm
1. Custer, George A. (George Armstrong), 1839–1876. 2. Generals—United States—Biography.
3. United States. Army—Biography. 4. United States—History—Civil War, 1861–1865.
5. Little Bighorn, Battle of the, Mont., 1876. 6. Indians of North America—Wars—Great Plains. I. Title.
E467.1.C99M4 2012
973.8'2092—dc23
[B]   2012012374
ISBN 978-1-4516-2620-9
ISBN 978-1-4516-2621-6 (pbk)
ISBN 978-1-4516-2622-3 (ebook)

Illustration credits will be found on page 177.

For Barbara Harris,
beloved helpmate

CUSTER

AT ONE TIME A PICTURE called *Custer's Last Stand* hung in virtually every saloon in the land, and quite a few barbershops too. I first saw it in our small barbershop, in Archer City, Texas. A painting by Cassilly Adams, lithographed by Otto Becker, was given away by the thousands by Anheuser-Busch, the great brewing enterprise of St. Louis: General George Armstrong Custer, long locks flying, was fighting on staunchly against terrible—in fact impossible—odds. And when he fell, along with some 250 of his men, the world was no longer the same.

Buffalo Bill Cody often used a skit called "Custer's Last Rally," as the finale of his Wild West Show, bringing the notion of long flowing locks and also the notion of a last stand to much of the civilized world. Adams's painting and Becker's lithograph are among the most famous images to come out of America. They brought the tragedy of the Little Bighorn alive to people not yet born.

George Armstrong Custer usually wore his hair long, but on the day of the famous battle— June 25, 1876—he sported a fresh haircut. The Indian who killed him—there are several candidates—may not immediately have known who they killed. But the women of the Sioux and Cheyenne, who soon came along and pierced Custer's eardrums with awls because he had disobeyed a perfectly clear warning from the Cheyenne chief Rock Forehead to respect the peace pipe, which Custer had smoked with him, knew exactly who they were working on. They were working on Long Hair,

whose hair just didn't happen to be long on the day he met his death.

By 1876, the year the Battle of the Little Bighorn was fought, the United States had become a nation of some forty million people, the vast majority of whom had never seen a fighting Indian—not, that is, unless they happened to glimpse one or another of the powerful Indian leaders whom the government periodically paraded through Washington or New York, usually Red Cloud, the powerful Sioux diplomat, who made a long-winded speech at Cooper Union in 1870. Or, it might be Spotted Tail, of the Brulé Sioux; or American Horse, or even, if they were lucky, Sitting Bull, who hated whites, the main exceptions being Annie Oakley, his "Little Sure Shot," or Buffalo Bill Cody, who once described Sitting Bull as "peevish," surely the understatement of the century. Sitting Bull often tried to marry Annie Oakley, who *was* married; he did not succeed.

The main purpose of this parading of Native American leaders—better not call them chiefs, not a title the red man accepted, or cared to use in their tribal life—was to overwhelm the Indians with their tall buildings, large cannon, and teeming masses, so they would realize the futility of further resistance. The Indians saw the point with perfect clarity, but continued to resist anyway. They were fighting for their culture, which was all they had.

One white who recognized this was the young cavalry officer George Armstrong Custer himself, who, in his flamboyant autobiography, *My Life on the Plains*, makes this point:

> If I were an Indian I think that I would greatly prefer to cast my lot with those of my people who adhered to the free life of the plains rather than to the limits of a reservation, there to be the recipient of the blessed benefits of civilization, with the vices thrown in without stint or measure.

Captain Frederick Benteen, who hated Custer and made no secret of it, called Custer's book *My Lie on the Plains*. Yet the book, despite its inaccuracies, is still readable today.

Ulysses S. Grant, who didn't like Custer either, had this to say about the dreadful loss of life at the Little Bighorn:

> I regard Custer's massacre as a sacrifice of troops, brought on by Custer himself, that was wholly unnecessary. . . . He was not to have made the attack before effecting the juncture with Generals Terry and Gibbon. Custer had been notified to meet them, but instead of marching slowly, as his orders required, in order to effect that juncture on the 26th, he entered upon a forced march of eighty-three miles in twenty-four hours, and thus had to meet the Indians alone.

That comment made Custer's widow, Libbie Custer, an enemy of Grant for life.

Thinking back on a number of important issues, Red Cloud of the Oglala Sioux made this comment: "The Whites made us many promises, more than I can remember," he said. "But they only kept one. They said they would take our land and they took it."

Crazy Horse, now thought by many to be the greatest Sioux warrior, refused to go to Washington. He didn't need to see tall buildings, big cannon, or teeming masses to know that his people's situation was dire. After the victory at the Little Bighorn the smart Indians all knew that they were playing an endgame. The white leaders—Crook, Miles,

RED CLOUD ADDRESSING A NEW YORK AUDIENCE.

Terry, Mackenzie—especially Mackenzie—were even so impolite as to fight in the dead of winter, something they didn't often do, although the Sioux Indians did wipe out the racist Captain Fetterman and his eighty men on the day of the winter solstice in 1866.

In Texas the so-called Red River War had ended in 1875 and some of its fighting talent, especially Ranald Slidell Mackenzie, went north to help out and *did* help out.

In the East and Midwest, as people became increasingly urbanized or suburbanized, these settled folk developed a huge appetite for stories of Western violence. Reportage suddenly surged; the *New York Times* and other major papers kept stringers all over the West, to report at once Sitting Bull's final resistance, or some mischief of Billy the Kid's or the Earps' revenge or any other signal violence that might have occurred. Publicity from the frontier helped keep Buffalo Bill's Wild West Show thriving. For a time the railroad bookstores groaned with dime novels describing Western deeds, the bloodier

LINCOLN MEETS CUSTER, OCT. 3, 1862, AT ANTIETAM.

the better. (See Richard Slotkin's masterpiece *The Fatal Environment* for a brilliant analysis of how the frontier affected our increasing urbanization.)

By Cody's day, indeed, the press had the power to make legends, names with an almost worldwide resonance. One of the legends that hasn't faded was that of the scruffy New Mexico outlaw Bill Bonney (one of several names he used), or Billy the Kid—no angel, it is true, but by no means the most deadly outlaw of his time. That was probably the sociopath John Wesley Hardin.

The other legend that remains very much alive is Custer's. The Battle of the Little Bighorn is considered by able historians to be one of the most important battles in world history, a claim we'll deal with in due course.

What Billy the Kid and Custer had in common was fighting; it's what we remember them for. Both died young, Billy the Kid at twenty-two and Custer at a somewhat weathered thirty-seven. Custer had barely managed to graduate from the military academy (34th out of 34) and then walked right into one of the biggest fights of all time, the American Civil War, a conflict in which 750,000 men lost their lives—warfare on a scale far different from the small-scale range wars that Billy the Kid engaged in.

In the Civil War, Custer's flair as a cavalry officer was immediately manifest; it found him at war's end the youngest major general in the U.S. Army. Custer's ambition, throughout his career, was furthered by the short, brusque General Philip Sheridan, of whom it was said that his head was so lumpy that he had trouble finding a hat that fit.

Not only did Custer have disciplinary problems at West Point, he continued to have

PHILIP HENRY SHERIDAN.

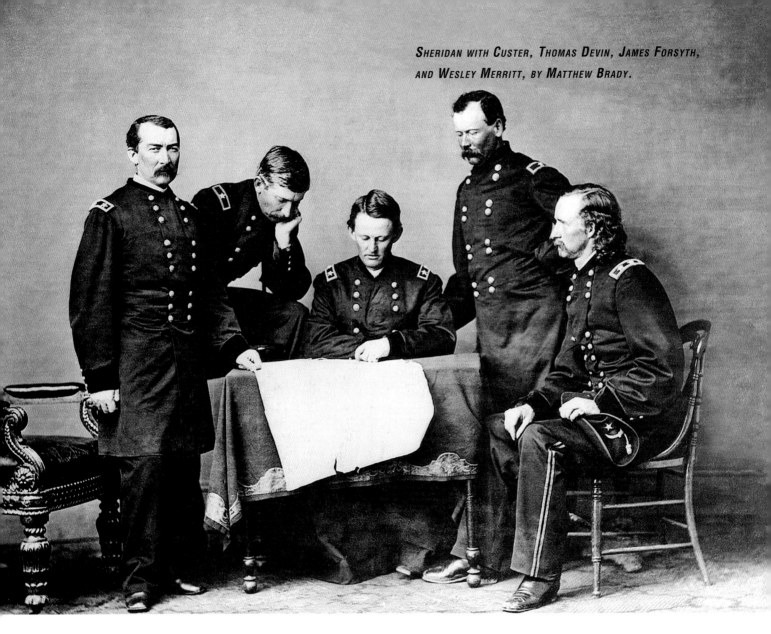

SHERIDAN WITH CUSTER, THOMAS DEVIN, JAMES FORSYTH, AND WESLEY MERRITT, BY MATTHEW BRADY.

disciplinary problems until the moment of his death, June 25, 1876. One thing was for sure: Custer *would* fight. Time after time his dash and aggression was rewarded, by Sheridan and others.

Ulysses Grant, also a man who would fight, came to distrust Custer—or maybe he just didn't like him. Grant was never convinced that Custer's virtues offset his liabilities.

Before the Battle of the Washita (1868), Custer was court-martialed on eight counts, the most serious being his abandonment of his command—he drifted off in search of his wife. He was convicted on all eight counts and put on the shelf for a year; though long before the year was up Sheridan was lobbying to get him back in the saddle.

To say that the literature on Custer—Custerology, Michael Elliott calls it, in a fine book of that name—is large would be to understate by a considerable measure. As a rare book dealer I once owned a collection of Custerology numbering more than one thousand items: scrapbooks, diaries, trial transcripts, regimental histories, publications of learned societies, reprints of reprints, and so on. And this collection was compiled long before the cyber-experts weighed in. It could easily be three times as large today, and the same could be said for the bibliography of Billy the Kid, which is now up there with Napoleon and Jesus when it comes to inflated coverage.

If the Battle of the Little Bighorn is rightly judged to be one of the most significant battles in history, then its significance comes from something other than body count.

The loss of life—about 250 men—was minute compared to the carnage of the Civil War, not to mention the terrible European battles of World War I and World War II. Yet even the stiff British military historian John Keegan considers the Little Bighorn to have been a major battle. I do too, because it closed a great narrative: the narrative of American settlement. I have just read four long books about Custer and his fate: Evan Connell's *Son of the Morning Star,* Robert Utley's *Cavalier in Buckskin,* James Donovan's *A Terrible Glory,* and Nathaniel Philbrick's *The Last Stand:* all of them are valuable books, but none of them says what I just said; at least they don't say it plainly. One reason I prefer the short life to the long life is that in the former plain speaking is usually required.

Another factor that these admirable books fail to stress is the element of surprise in the outcome of the battle itself. The Indians had not expected the whites to attack when they were gathered in such numbers, and Custer, despite vehement warnings from scouts and colleagues, still expected the Indians to run, not fight. And, again, despite all the warnings, Custer just did not expect to find so many Indians.

Surprise, surprise, you're dead!

Several times, over the years, I have been asked to write a life of Custer, and have declined mainly because I found Evan Connell's *Son of the Morning Star* to be a masterpiece that is unlikely to be bettered: a literary mosaic on the one hand and a feat of literary archaeology on the other, with Connell working patiently in the inexhaustible dig of the Little Bighorn, where he frequently unearths shards of commentary that no one else has found.

In my recent rereading of the book, I found it still brilliant but with perhaps too many shards of commentary. Thanks to all the Native American memories that have emerged in recent decades, it is possible to wind up with a great many shards, some of only distant relevance to the main question. So one corpse had 105 arrows in him? So what?

There are a number of historians who believe that history's great enigmas should be revisited by each successive generation in turn. These revisitings may produce new insights and possibly lead to new conclusions. Maybe that's true, or maybe it's just an excuse to write more about Custer. It's been twenty-five years since Connell's book was published, years during which much has happened in the world that once was Custer's and his foes'.

I was attracted to the notion of a short life of Custer in part because the short life is itself a lovely form, a form that once was common in English letters: there's Henry James on Hawthorne, Rebecca West on Augustine, Nabokov on Gogol, Edmund White on Proust, and myself on Crazy Horse.

No matter what I write here, Custer's fights will continue to engage historians. One of the duties of the short life is to bring clarity to the subject. A historian, of course, can be clear and wrong, but clarity, in my view, is the one thing the historian or biographer owes his or her reader. I hope I can achieve it here.

COMANCHE MEETING THE DRAGOONS, 1834.

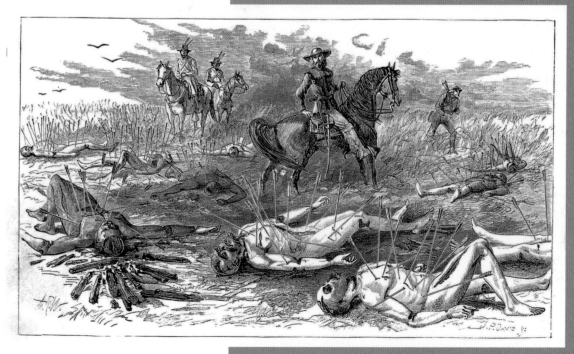

THE KIDDER MURDER.

CHEYENNE INDIANS
ATTACK UNION PACIFIC
RAILROAD WORKERS.

COMANCHE VILLAGE *BY*
GEORGE CATLIN.

BEFORE DISCUSSING CUSTER'S YOUTH I would like to address a matter that has not, it seems to me, been significantly factored into the narrative of Western settlement, and that is the confusion of tongues that prevailed in the West during the whole period of settlement.

What's clear is that there was, from the first, a serious shortage of really competent translators. The well-known example of Crazy Horse is a good example of how things can go if the translator is not up to snuff.

Crazy Horse surrendered on May 6, 1877, a surrender that drew lavish coverage from the Eastern press. Sometime after the surrender the army learned that it had a problem with the fleeing Nez Perce, an Idaho tribe, which was on its way to Canada, killing most everyone who strayed into its path.

The army didn't like Crazy Horse—General George Crook was planning to ship him to the prison for incorrigibles in Florida—but somebody decided he might be useful against the Nez Perce. So, having just taken his rifle, they offered it back to him if he would use it to fight the Nez Perce. Crazy Horse knew little about the Nez but allowed as how he would happily go kill them all.

The main translator that day was a sometime friend of Crazy Horse named Frank Grouard, a scout of part Polynesian descent. Grouard had Crazy Horse saying he would go kill all the *white people* if they wanted him to.

This set the army against him of course, and his own people were already against him: he had become too famous. Soon after this odd business he was bayoneted by a soldier at Fort Robinson, Nebraska, while Little Big Man, another former friend, held his arms. He would have been killed by his own people had the soldier not gotten there first. The Indians were—and are—very jealous of their own. Success in the white world doesn't carry well.

The mistranslation of Crazy Horse's statement is not only famous—it's typical. At powwow after powwow the two sides came away believing something different. This

GRAND COUNCIL AT FORT LARAMIE.

occurred at the first big Western peace conference at Laramie in 1851, and had occurred even earlier at a powwow with Comanches and Kiowa. George Catlin painted many of the Comanches at this council and his paintings probably provide the most accurate record of that gathering of peoples.

The reasons for the sloppy translations are many. For one thing, the native languages are rather hard. They don't easily fit into the white man's conceptual world. And the translators were often fringe people: scouts, squaw men, trappers, half-breeds, soldiers. Exact agreement was almost impossible. The writer Alex Shoumatoff says the United States has broken around 350 treaties with the Indians—all we made, in fact. None achieved linguistic perfection, though it got better once Carlisle Indian School linguists began to serve as translators.

For much of the settlement period the most effective speech was not speech at all, it was sign. Most frontiersmen were fluent in sign, and many more had at least a tentative grasp of it. A famous example of it exists in the often quoted remarks of the Crow scout Half Yellow Face, made to Custer just before the end. *All* the scouts, without exception, warned Custer that he would die if he rode down into the valley of the Little Bighorn, but the most poetic warning came from Half Yellow Face, who remarked that "today we will all go home by a road we do not know." At least he was quoted as having said that.

But what language did he make this famous statement in? He spoke no English, and Custer spoke no Crow. (Elizabeth—Libbie—Custer claimed that Custer spoke fluent Cheyenne, but no one who fought with him agreed, or had ever heard his Cheyenne.) Could Half Yellow Face have conveyed this metaphor in sign?

In any case much trouble resulted from this confusion of tongues. All treaties were somewhat flawed, and many were absurd. The most immediately revoked, probably, was the famous treaty of 1868 in which we gave the Black Hills to the Sioux in perpetuity, which turned out to be only about five years. Rumors of gold in those dark, dangerous hills quickly proved to be true, thus presaging a war with the Sioux, who were to win two significant victories: against Crook at the Rosebud and against Custer at the Little Bighorn.

Myself, I find it easy to doubt much of what's been said, or reported as said, by the various scouts to Custer as the battle thickened. Custer divided his companies into three, making communication difficult, if not impossible.

Particularly doubtful, in my opinion, is the famous cry "Hurrah boys, we've got them," which Custer is supposed to have uttered when he saw the Indians. By the time he would have delivered this famous cry he must have known that something close to the reverse was true: they had him.

Indeed, by all reports, Custer entered this campaign without his usual bravado. On the morning of his departure from Fort Lincoln he was said to be subdued. Usually he was stimulated at the prospects of a fight.

When, with the battle nearly joined, his old enemy Benteen suggested politely that it might be best not to break up the troop, Custer merely said, "You have your orders."

At least seven or eight native languages were spoken by participants in this battle. Their names, when they surfaced in white man's parlance, would have surprised those participants if they had lived long enough to see them on marquees. Crazy Horse, Curly in his youth, was in tribal life Tashunca-uitco (Dancing Horse, Magical Horse), while Tatanka-Iyotanka was the tribal name for Sitting Bull. Both Sitting Bull and Geronimo learned to sign their marquee names, though even today few Apaches will tell you Geronimo's tribal name: Goyakla, one who yawns, close, maybe, to the Spanish Jerome.

The tribal people believed, rightly perhaps, that giving a person your name gave him a certain power over you. And complicating the issue was the fact that the Indians sometimes held two names at the same time. Rock Forehead, the Cheyenne chief who warned Custer about going against the peace pipe, was also called Medicine Arrows, because he was the keeper of the sacred tribal arrows. The visit when this warning was given was just after the Battle of the Washita; Custer had been sent to soothe Cheyenne feelings, which he signally failed to do.

5

THE LATE HISTORIAN STEPHEN AMBROSE wrote a book on Crazy Horse and Custer in which he traced the parallels between the careers of these two famous warriors: the impetuous cavalryman and the elusive Oglala.

There is another man whose career has some uncanny parallels with Custer's: the explorer and topographer John Charles Frémont, known popularly as the Pathfinder, though, in fact, he found few paths. He claimed, for example, to have discovered South Pass, the famous gateway through the Rockies that led to Oregon and California. In fact this route was used by the Overland Astorians well before Frémont, was well known to mountain men and trappers, and, of course, was used by the Indians forever. Frémont didn't "find" it until he first went west in 1842.

CUSTER AND CRAZY HORSE FIGHTING *BY* KILLS TWO.

Frémont was trained as a topographer by the fine French student of landscape Joseph Nicollet, who achieved immortality, of a sort, through television. When Mary Tyler Moore, working girl of Minneapolis, flings her cap in the air while she is walking to work, she is standing in what is now Nicollet Mall.

Like Custer, Frémont had early success. Custer's cavalry work during the Civil War made him a hero, whereas Frémont's reports on his first two Western expeditions made him one of the most popular authors of his day.

Like Custer, Frémont married—indeed eloped with—an impressive and ambitious woman, Jesse Benton Frémont, daughter of Senator Thomas Hart Benton, of Missouri.

When things went south for the General, as Jesse called her husband, Jesse leapt to his defense, just as did Libbie Custer when her George, whom she also called General, was attacked from all sides. Libbie defended Custer for more than fifty years.

JOHN CHARLES FRÉMONT.

Early glory and lively wives were not the only things that Custer and Frémont had in common: another shared attribute was the ability to get so far and no farther. Custer never became a Grant, nor Frémont a Jefferson. Frémont's high-water mark came in 1846, while leading his third expedition, which was more or less the reverse of what his orders charged him to do. In this he was just like Custer: orders meant nothing.

Frémont's intent, on the third expedition, was simply to annex the whole of California, though at the time it belonged to Mexico.

At this point a high destiny seemed well within Frémont's grasp; but then, as the historian Bernard DeVoto put it, things began to go ever so subtly wrong, just as they went less subtly wrong for George Armstrong Custer.

Frémont, mind you, had genuine gifts as a topographer. He saw, understood, and named the Great Basin; and he even managed to eliminate a ghost river that was supposed to cross the Sierras but didn't. He also named the Golden Gate, and may have been the first person to suggest that the Napa Valley might be a fine place to grow grapes.

Frémont's troubles came because he was naive about politics; Custer's difficulties were usually the result of carelessness. His abandonment of Major Joel Elliott and eighteen of his men at the Battle of the Washita—supposedly his one great victory against the plains Indians—turned the entire officer corps against him. Many of them testified against him at his court-martial. Most of these officers were his own age: as his career went, so did theirs.

MAJOR JOEL ELLIOTT.

Frémont, for his part, went so far as to defy the authority of General Stephen Watts Kearny, who had been sent west to drive out the Mexicans, after which he would run California as a territory. Frémont fatally misjudged Kearny's mettle: Kearny took him back to Washington and court-martialed him. Like Custer he was convicted on various counts, including mutiny, and this despite desperate lobbying on the part of Jesse and her father.

Custer's gall was also massive. After the Washita he found that he missed his wife, and simply rode off in search of her. She finally turned up in Fort Riley, Kansas.

Frémont made mistakes involving the security of his men that were very much in the Custer mode. On his disastrous fourth expedition he proposed to survey a railroad line through the heart of the Rockies in midwinter. This was mainly to please his father-in-law, who owned a home on the 39th parallel and reasoned that it would be a fine place for a railroad.

Frémont's favorite guide on his first three expeditions was the very experienced Kit Carson, who was not available (or perhaps not willing), so Frémont took instead the rascally mountain man Old Bill Williams, of whom Kit Carson said: "Nobody who knows him walks ahead of Bill Williams in the starving times." On this trip Williams failed to get them through the massif. Ten of Frémont's men died in the mountains: it was his Little Bighorn. He himself retreated to Kit Carson's home in Taos; he wrote his wife how pleasant it was to be in Kit Carson's snug house, sipping hot chocolate as the winter deepened. Meanwhile the starving times had come for his men. Old Bill Williams survived the chill but was soon dispatched by a party of Utes, his mortal enemies, whom he had defrauded many times.

Frémont had done exactly what Custer was to do: abandoned his men to a cruel and unnecessary death.

Both men had genuine abilities and had the good sense to play to their strengths. The maps that were published with Frémont's reports were useful to travelers in the Rockies for decades to come. Regrettably he never bothered to do his final assignment, which was to survey the rivers flowing east out of the Rockies, particularly the Arkansas and the Red.

Custer, of course, did not live to grow old, but Frémont, a very handsome man, seemed to grow more handsome as he grew sadder.

Abraham Lincoln apparently let Frémont's splendid appearance convince him that he was a soldier, which he was not. Lincoln gave him two important assignments—the Department of Missouri, for one—and Frémont immediately flubbed both of them, losing both territory and men. Lincoln finally shuttled him off to West Virginia; rather than serve under General John Pope, Frémont resigned.

The final parallel with Custer was political ambition. Frémont had it and took it nearly to the presidency. How politically ambitious Custer was is hard to say. He may have told some Indian that he would be the next White Father: we'll never know.

Frémont, though, was a better than fair politician. In 1856, though losing to James Buchanan, he made a good showing. The Radical Republicans ran him again in 1864 but he pulled out due to lack of funds. He made money for a while, but rarely kept it. Given a fine home in California, he and Jesse soon had to sell it. They were often bankrupt and the General was even convicted of bank fraud in France.

Within the military structure Custer was undoubtedly ambitious. He left Fort Abraham Lincoln bitter that the overall command had been given to General Alfred Terry rather than himself. He may not have realized that he was not a particularly good Indian fighter, though the term Indian fighter would always be linked to him. He was much better at fighting his Civil War foes, who had trained in the same disciplines, at the same schools. But the Indians fought in a different way, and Custer never really got himself prepared for it.

Which man had the sadder lot is not easy to say. Custer's life was abruptly snuffed out by two Sioux or Cheyenne bullets. Almost every venture Frémont undertook failed. He philandered endlessly—Jesse grew fat and sad. He died while doing a friend a favor—he brought some flowers and placed them on a grave in Brooklyn. The grave was the friend of a friend. He would have done better to have stuck to his first love, topography; he had a real aptitude for landscapes. But, as a mere mapmaker, could he have attracted Jesse? He tried for glory and found a little bit of it.

6

George Armstrong Custer was of Hessian stock, Custer being probably a corruption of Kuester. Until he arrived at West Point his life was almost entirely rural. He was born in New Rumley, Ohio, and was raised there and in Monroe, Michigan. His father, Emmanuel, was a farmer and a blacksmith. Eventually there were twelve in his family, death and remarriage achieving that total.

Custer had many failings, but lack of family feeling was not among them. He loved his brother Tom, and his stepsister Lydia Kirkpatrick, the only living human to exercise much control over the boy or the man.

CUSTER AT SIXTEEN.

MATTHEW BRADY PORTRAIT
OF LIBBIE CUSTER.

In a famous episode while he was courting Libbie Bacon he showed up on her doorstep very drunk and loudly profane. Lydia was visiting and proceeded to tear into him with such force that he was never known to touch liquor again.

His beloved brother Tom Custer died with him at the Little Bighorn, as did his brother Boston, a nephew, and a stepbrother.

He also deeply loved his mother. Their partings were terrible. Libbie, once she be-

TOM CUSTER.

came a daughter-in-law, found them almost intolerable; she dreaded accompanying her husband on his trips home.

Custer's first biographer was an English dime novelist named Frederick Whittaker; his primary virtue was that he wrote fast. He began his book while Custer was still alive and managed to kick it into print by the end of 1876. If Custer read even a small sampling of it he probably laughed his head off: Whittaker was to Custer as Parson Weems was to Washington. (The great editor Milo Milton Quaife was the first to make that observation.)

GEORGE CUSTER.

GEORGE ARMSTRONG CUSTER HAD UNUSUALLY perfect timing as he moved from one stage of his career to another, the exception being June 25, 1876, when his timing could not have been worse.

West Point itself he seemed to treat as a lively teenager might a summer camp: a good place to have fun. His academic record was dismal, and his demerits numerous; he finished 34th out of 34.

But another example of his timing was that he matriculated in the class of 1861, which allowed him to be shoveled right into the Army of the Potomac. (He fought in the first battle of the Civil War, and also in the last.)

The Civil War made Custer: for him it was four years of sport. Nowhere does he mention the 750,000 dead, or the agony of the field hospitals, the shattered nation, the husbandless widows, the childless mothers, their best hope buried; a great national tragedy that left many promising lives unlived. In that war the world got the first taste of the destructive power of modern weaponry, the great war engines that showed their full power fifty years later, in the carnage of World War I and later World War II.

But Custer was lucky, given his talents, to have the perfect war waiting for him when he graduated.

When he began to demonstrate his flare, the generals he was then introduced to were astonished at first by his youth. George McClellan called him a "mere boy." Custer hung around West Point until mid-June, arriving in Washington just in time to fight in the Battle of Bull Run. He was very active during the whole conflict, bringing in the first prisoner by the 5th Cavalry; and, years later, seeing a rebel soldier holding a towel as a signal of surrender, he came in with one of the last.

And Custer's dash and flare were genuine, besides which they made the generals look good, Sheridan particularly.

Barely mentioned by historians is the dark side of Custer's war: the execution with-

CUSTER AFTER THE
BATTLE OF FIVE FORKS.

out trial of Confederate guerrillas. Sheridan asked him to do this, and he did it without noticeable loss of sleep.

A famous story from the war has Custer chasing a Confederate on a fine thoroughbred; he rode an ornate saddle and was also carrying an expensive sword. Custer, after

LIEUTENANT JAMES BARROLL AND SECOND LIEUTENANT CUSTER, MAY 31, 1862.

asking him twice to surrender, killed him, keeping the horse, the saddle, and the sword. When taxed about the ethics of the matter, Custer always said it was the rebel's fault; after all, he had asked twice.

HARPER'S WEEKLY.

A JOURNAL OF CIVILIZATION.

Vol. VIII.—No. 411.]   NEW YORK, SATURDAY, NOVEMBER 12, 1864.   [SINGLE COPIES TEN CENTS.
[$4.00 PER YEAR IN ADVANCE.

Entered according to Act of Congress, in the Year 1864, by Harper & Brothers, in the Clerk's Office of the District Court for the Southern District of New York.

SHERIDAN'S VICTORY.

WE give in the subjoined illustration a representation of the highly interesting ceremony in which General CUSTER officiated, on Sunday, October 23—namely, that of presenting to the Secretary of War the Battle-Flags captured from the Rebels in the Battle of Cedar Creek. General CUSTER arrived in Washington on the Saturday before the ceremony took place; and ten of the captured flags were displayed from the railroad engine as the train came in. During the presentation it was announced that General CUSTER had been appointed Major-General, and this fact occasioned great enthusiasm among the large crowd assembled to witness the ceremony.

One of the colors captured was the head-quarters flag of the late rebel General RAMSEUR, bearing the inscription, "On to Victory! Presented by Mr. W. T. Sutherlin." A large number of the colors were taken by CUSTER's Division. General RAMSEUR was a class-mate of General CUSTER's at West Point, and as the former was dying the two reviewed together the reminiscences of their cadet life.

FORGING SOLDIERS' VOTES.

WE give on page 725 a sketch showing the manner in which the Copperheads obtain their votes. The facts of the case, at its present development,

are as follows: The first suspicion that something wrong was going on in regard to the soldiers' vote in this State occurred to Mr. ORVILLE K. WOOD, who was in the army procuring votes in behalf of the Union Committee of Clinton County. Proceeding thereupon to the agency of the State of New York at Baltimore, and gaining the confidence of a certain Mr. FERRY, the agent appointed by Governor SEYMOUR two years ago to look after sick and wounded soldiers in and around Baltimore, he found his suspicions more than confirmed. Mr. FERRY remarked to Mr. WOOD that when Union votes came to that office "they went out all right." In Mr. WOOD's presence this Mr. FERRY and his fellow-agents, DONAHUE, NEW-

COMB, and others, signed soldiers' names to votes, filling out the blanks with other names in regular order, all forged; altered Union votes, so that soldiers giving their suffrages to Mr. LINCOLN were made to vote for General M'CLELLAN, and affixed to Democratic ballots the names of sick and wounded, and even of dead soldiers. The conspirators admitted that a number of agents were employed in a similar manner, and that soldiers' votes were in this way manufactured by the dry-goods' box full. These statements are sworn to in court by two of those engaged in the fraud, and the exhibition of the documents, consisting of a number of the forged votes, and a large amount of correspondence, leaves no room for doubt as to the nature and

GENERAL CUSTER PRESENTING CAPTURED BATTLE-FLAGS AT THE WAR DEPARTMENT, WASHINGTON, OCTOBER 23, 1864.—[SKETCHED BY A. R. WAUD.]

HARPER'S WEEKLY: CUSTER PRESENTS CAPTURED BATTLE FLAGS.

CUSTER, HIS BROTHER TOM, AND WIFE, LIBBIE.

CUSTER CIRCA *1863.*

CUSTER ON HIS WEDDING DAY.

CUSTER WITH BEARD, *1868.*

CUSTER WITH HIS HORSE, COMANCHE.

CUSTER WAS FAR FROM BEING a gracious or easy commander of men. On marches he stayed aloof, or with his officers, making little effort to promote camaraderie. Though his general's rank was brevet, meaning temporary, he soon began to behave as if it were permanent. He insisted on traveling with a cook, which meant a cookstove, which caused many delays. He generally favored black cooks, though on the Black Hills/Yellowstone expedition of 1873 he took a white cook.

After Custer's abandonment of Major Joel Elliott and his men on the Washita, very few officers wanted much to do with him, though most of them liked Libbie—Captain Benteen being an exception.

Early in the Custers' marriage they were sent to Texas. The War Department was a little worried about Mexico, where the drama of Maximilian was being played out. The trip is worth mentioning because of Custer's utter disregard of civilized behavior. Libbie was carried to her buggy in the morning so that the heavy East Texas dew would not wet her fine slippers. The Custers ate well but the men were starving. Two who killed and cooked a crippled calf were flogged for their temerity. What Libbie thought of this is not recorded.

If Custer signally lacked something it was what the rest of the world calls conscience. He had no capacity for empathizing with the pain and suffering of others.

Conditions being what they were, desertion was a constant problem, both in Texas or Kansas, sometimes running as high as 50 percent. Custer treated the deserters savagely, often sending his brother Tom to shoot them. Those who made it back to the forts faced cruel punishment.

Grant saw through Custer, though he did acknowledge that the man would fight. Grant would fight and so would Lee. Auchinleck didn't, at least not enough to satisfy his boss, Winston Churchill.

If one happened to be in a war, the Custer model was useful, especially if maturity could somehow be injected into the model. The "mere boy" McClellan saw in 1862 was just as single-minded in 1876—only then he was in the position to lose the lives of 250 men, which is essentially what he did.

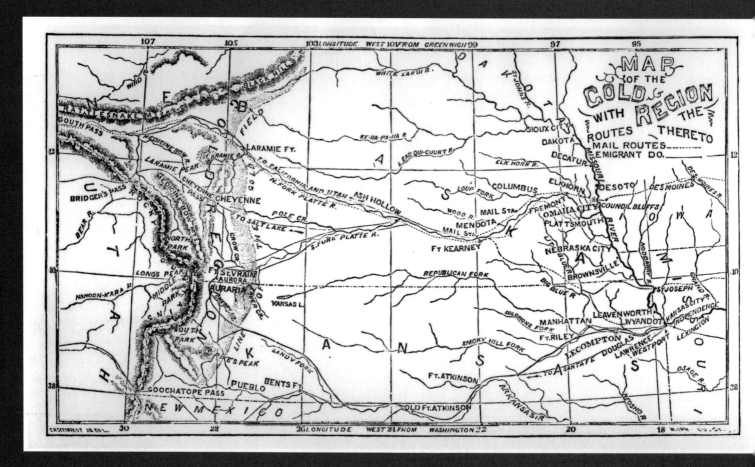

Since much of Custer's career concerned itself with the plains Indians, it might be worth sketching in the political context in which he worked, 1860 to 1875 or thereabouts.

In the decade of the 1840s immigration along various routes began to increase rapidly. All of a sudden it was Oregon or bust, and quite a few did bust. Frémont's report on his first expedition to the Rockies in 1842 prompted settlers to set out for the glorious West. The report spoke of what he claimed to be his great find, South Pass, and told of rafting mountain rivers in his famous rubber boat. The California Gold Rush, coming just at the end of the decade, increased immigration tenfold. Diseases spread by the Forty-niners decimated some of the Indian tribes, the Comanche-Kiowa peoples particularly.

The lure of gold proved irresistible. Along the Platte River, the Oregon Trail—called by Indians the Holy Road—took tens of thousands west. Overland guidebooks, on the order of Captain Randolph Marcy's *The Prairie Traveler*, soon began to flourish, guiding immigrants from one water hole to the next. Some of these guides, many of them printed on small local presses, are worth their weight in gold today. The immigrants could hardly wait to harvest the plenty they knew to be in Oregon, but, unhappily for these newcomers, there existed a large and hostile group of people who didn't want them to get there at all, the so-called plains Indians, who were appalled as wagon train after wagon train crossed what they had supposed to be their land. These people lived communally, fed by the overabundant buffalo, and they liked it that way. Soon, though, to their astonishment, even the buffalo began to change their migration patterns so as to avoid being shot by the powerful rifles of the invaders.

The plains Indians were very gifted hunter-gatherers. As long as they had the buffalo they were about as secure as nomads can be. They were understandably furious about the wagon trains, and their fury vented itself on the whites, many of whom were not only killed but mutilated in inventive ways. The whites were horrified: they were used to fighting but not to butchery. The government decided that something must be done, so the head soldiers decided to try a council, which had worked fairly well with

SHERMAN AT TREATY OF FORT LARAMIE WITH RED CLOUD.

the Senecas and Mohawks and other Eastern Indians; Fort Laramie, on the Platte, was made the site of this famous council and the year was 1851. The big question was whether the plains Indians would actually come. There had been one big Western council, held in what is now Oklahoma. George Catlin painted many of the Comanches who showed up at this one at Fort Laramie.

The white leaders need not have worried about attendance at Fort Laramie. The Indians came by the thousands, riding their best horses and all their finery, in the way of bear claws and eagle feathers.

The whites were not a retiring people: the Indians soon realized that these scoundrels wanted it all, the buffalo, the grasslands, the minerals; and they particularly wanted to achieve safe passage along the Platte, for which they were willing to pay the Indians a modest annuity.

How well the Indians understood this offer is hard to say. They knew it was money, of some sort, but would the whites keep their word? The Indians displayed themselves grandly, so grandly that the more intelligent of the whites probably realized that the plains Indians were a problem that was not going to go away anytime soon.

A generational divide began to display itself among these tribal peoples: the older warriors wanted to get paid, the younger warriors wanted to fight. Black Kettle, the Cheyenne chief whom Custer would kill, said many times what while he loved peace he could not control his young men, who had been trained from birth in a warrior culture: they would fight, no matter what. They were scornful of ambushes, although they held one well when they destroyed Fetterman in 1868.

Custer would have understood this instinctively, which is not to suggest that he made any special study of the tribes he engaged. He was trained in a warrior society himself.

What the young men of the plains tribes wanted was to continue fighting, as their fathers had fought. Not for them were trips to Washington and New York. Leave that to Red Cloud and Spotted Tail.

What they wanted was to attack a wagon train and kill all the whites in it, just as their fathers had done.

WHILE THE CIVIL WAR HELD the nation's attention, the Indian problem was mostly put on hold. Custer demonstrated his brilliance as a cavalry officer while white-Indian relations, in most places, were coming to a boil. One of these places was Minnesota, where a well-established immigrant route west from the Mississippi was functioning well. But, in 1862, the Santee Sioux, under Little Crow, promptly unestablished this popular route, the reason for the war being that the Sioux were being starved by crooked contractors. These contractors were supposed to give the Sioux corn but withheld the corn until they could pocket their own stipends. One contractor named Myrick said that if the Sioux were hungry they could eat grass or their own excrement: when the Sioux killed Mr. Myrick they stuffed his mouth with grass.

It took the army a while to put down this rebellion, by which time immigration on that stretch of the Mississippi had been much reduced.

Little Crow had been against the uprising, but he was not needed. The army eventually subdued the Sioux and, mindful of public outrage, built gallows enough to hang three hundred men; and would have had not President Lincoln carefully reviewed the files and reduced the number to be hanged to thirty-three.

What the Indians had to face, in the 1860s and 1870s, was that the whites were not going to back off. Many more whites were killed in messy ways and yet the wagon trains kept coming.

One of the whites who was in the business of protecting the immigrants was George Armstrong Custer. But he worked for a nation suffering from considerable war weariness. Thousands of shattered families had their lives to put back together. Mothers didn't want to send their sons into yet more battles—and who could blame them?

To the surprise and disgust of the soldiers who had actually fought Indians and had seen what they did to captives, a Peace Party began to form, some of whose members had some political clout. President Grant, in his heart, probably sided with the soldiers,

ATTENTION!
INDIAN
FIGHTERS

Having been authorized by the Governor to raise a
Company of 100 day

U. S. VOL CAVALRY!

For immediate service against hostile Indians. I call upon all who wish to engage in such
service to call at my office and enroll their names immediately.

Pay and Rations the same as other U. S.
Volunteer Cavalry.

Parties furnishing their own horses will receive 40c per day, and rations for the same,
while in the service.
The Company will also be entitled to all horses and other plunder taken from the Indians.

Office first door East of Recorder's Office.
HAL SAYR.

Central City, Aug. 13, '64.

but he had more problems to deal with than he could readily handle. He appointed a decent secretary of the interior, J. D. Cox, and left many of these problems to him.

The Peace Party itself was made up of a miscellaneous collection of do-gooders: Quakers, former abolitionists, reformers of every stamp. The nation was divided into zones, each group controlling a zone. The Quakers got the agency in Indian Territory—what we now call Oklahoma—where they quickly learned that if there is one thing the Indians particularly despise it is farming. The influential Sioux warrior Young Man Afraid of His Horses angrily reckoned that he might learn to farm if he had one hundred years—and what, in the meantime, were his people to eat?

Probably the bitterest opponent of the Peace Policy was the shrewd and brilliant William Tecumseh Sherman, a frank and outspoken exterminationist. In his view the Indians had to go, and the sooner the better. When Grant put him over the Division of

WILLIAM TECUMSEH SHERMAN.

the Mississippi (the West) Grant had the power to effect some change; what he didn't have, yet, was money. He simply didn't have the muscle to overpower the Sioux and Cheyenne.

Sherman, probably the smartest man in Grant's government, placed his ultimate hopes on the railroads. Once the Northern Pacific was pushed through—a task Custer aided by guarding one of the surveying crews—the buffalo would soon be hunted out and the Indians with them: the tribal peoples would either accept reservation life, or die.

Custer, I think, mostly agreed with Grant. In his autobiography he writes scornfully of the Peace Party—in particular he condemns the foolish practice of giving the Indians rifles. At the Medicine Lodge parley in 1867 the Indians were given Lancaster rifles, heavy guns which were useful in killing buffalo. The people who were giving the Indians these guns were not the soldiers in the field. Political pressure was soon applied, and dispensing guns to the Indians soon ceased, although they continued to secure many through various trades.

CHIEF GALL.

Custer, who rarely saw an Indian who wouldn't have liked to kill him, heaped much scorn on the Peace Party for their unrealistic views.

His wife, Libbie, also didn't like Indians, though some years after her husband's death she was introduced to the undeniably impressive Sioux leader Gall, a much wounded survivor of the Little Bighorn. Libbie was stunned, and testified willingly to Gall's superb bearing and ability.

In the fall of 1864, an event occurred which outraged all the plains Indians and a goodly number of whites too.

This was the Sand Creek Massacre, an attack on a peaceful Cheyenne village in southern Colorado led by the mad preacher John Chivington. The attack was made on the village of Black Kettle, probably the leading peace Indian of his day, who frantically waved an American flag as his people were being slaughtered.

JOHN M. CHIVINGTON.

THE ONLY CHILD SAVED FROM THE SAND CREEK MASSACRE.

THE MASSACRE OF INDIANS IN COLORADO.

A letter from Maj. CALLEY, United States Indian Agent,
is as follows:

"DECEMBER 20, 1864.

"I was in hopes our Indian troubles were over. I had
two hundred and fifty lodges near this place under my protection and that of Fort Lyon. All the chiefs and their
families were in camp and doing all they could to protect
the whites and keep the peace, when Col. Chivington
marched from Denver, surprised the village, killed one-
half of them, all the women and children, and then returned to Denver. Few if any white men can now live if an
Indian can kill them.

"Fort Lyon is on the direct road from the States to
Santa Fe and the commerce of the plains is millions each
year. Chivington took six hundred ponies, which were
loaded down with plunder on his return.

Headquarters, Department of Kansas.

Fort Leavenworth, Jany 13 1865

clip a scrap from the Intelligencer
is probably a part of the occasion
of General Hallecks order concerning an investigation
of the conduct of Col Chivington. I suppose a
Commission of officers better be ordered and have so
telegraphed you. I have also attached Fort
Lyon to your command so as to accommodate the
matter. If the Colonel did attack that
Camp knowing it to be under the instructions
of the Commander at Lyons or the Indian Agent
he committed a grave error and may have very
much embarrassed our Indian affairs. But I
have written General Halleck that such reports
must be taken with great allowance. I desire
that a fair and full exposure of the facts be made.

Maj Mc Nett is absent and I cannot therefore
get his order concerning Arms: but if a
great necessity arises I trust you will order
the Ordnance officer to issue and he must
act upon your order in view of the necessity
and he will be justified. I suppose

Chivington was at that time based in Denver, a city that had more reason than most to worry about outrages and depredations from the red men, due to the fact that east of town was an open prairie stretching several hundreds of miles. Any whites who crossed it—and many did, particularly after gold was discovered in Colorado—were vulnerable to attack, on a plain where there was virtually no cover to be had.

There were many attacks. The young men of the plains tribes liked nothing better than to set fire to a wagon train or kill a few gold rushers. Black Kettle was not the only chief who could not control his young men—he was just one of the few to admit it.

Chivington wouldn't have spared that village, no matter how peaceful it was. He wanted nothing more than to kill Indians—to wade in gore, as he bluntly put it. He raised perhaps one thousand men and launched his raid at dawn on November 29, 1864. Considering the size of the force that came down on them, it is surprising that *any* Indians survived, but a few did, escaping along Sand Creek.

Some of the military men who rode with the raiders were not happy to find that they were being asked to take part in a slaughter of historic proportions. One young officer, Lieutenant Silas Soule, refused to fight and testified against Chivington at the

THE SAND CREEK TELEGRAM.

inquiry that the brutality of the action made necessary. Lieutenant Soule was later murdered while walking on a summer's night with his bride. Passions ran high on both sides, and, for that matter, still do. I have been to Sand Creek and find it, like several other massacre sites, a haunting place.

Black Kettle's wife received nine wounds at Sand Creek, but Black Kettle carried her to Fort Lyon and she lived, only to be finished off by Custer on the Washita. Sand Creek was very brutal; on a stage in Denver, Chivington exhibited one hundred Cheyenne scalps, and some pudenda, to wild cheers.

It was then twelve years to the Little Bighorn. Elizabeth was now trying to adjust to army life, with its many vexations. She was not a complainer, despite living in Kansas and North Dakota, two of the bleakest places in the West. About the worst aggravation she would admit to was that one of her husband's stag hounds wanted to be her lapdog, which did not make for a very good fit.

THIS STAG HOUND WAS BUT one of the many critters that Elizabeth Custer had to put up with. Custer loved animals and they loved him. At one point he even had a pet antelope. He liked big rangy dogs, dogs that could keep up with him as he loped around the plains on a hunt. As a budding general, Custer had quickly adapted himself to living high, a lifestyle he found hard to give up once his rank dropped back to where it had been. He was a captain for a while, and then, in Kansas, a lieutenant colonel.

This is when he began to consider being a mercenary in Mexico. Quite a few bored veterans of the Civil War took this route. The United States had handily whipped Mexico in the war of 1846–48, and afterward gained a huge amount of territory in the Treaty of Guadalupe Hildago: Texas, New Mexico, Arizona, California, with the Gadsden Purchase coming a little later.

In Custer's time the fear was that Mexico was falling under French influence—this was because of the foolish, doomed, sad emperorship of young Maximilian, brother to the Hapsburg Franz Joseph. The real ruler of Mexico was the flintlike Benito Juárez, who tightened the screws on Maximilian whenever he saw fit. The final screw, the young man's execution, came in 1867.

It seems doubtful that Ulysses Grant lost much sleep over Mexico—no action was taken nor threats issued: the only consequence, for our story, is that Custer got sent to Texas, as described. The complete indifference that Custer displayed on that strange journey—indifference to the suffering of his troops—was to reappear in spades at the Little Bighorn. He did not consider that an eighty-three-mile forced march might put his weary troops at a disadvantage when they finally had to face what had frequently been described to him as a huge mass of Indians. The battle plan in his own head was all that mattered to him, and by the time he sensed his folly it was too late.

CUSTER WITH HIS DOG.

IN 1867, WHEN THE GOVERNMENT had to think seriously about the Indian problem, there were two broad propulations to be reckoned with before white settlement would be safe. These populations, like the buffalo herds they depended upon, were roughly divided between a northern group and a southern. The north belonged to the Sioux, the northern Cheyenne, the Blackfeet, among others, whereas to the south were the southern Cheyenne, the Comanche-Kiowa, and various smaller tribes such as the Kickapoo.

Sherman, Sheridan, and various other generals realized that, for a time, the war-weary, impoverished army simply was not up to whipping the northern tribes, so, barely, maybe, they could prevail against the southern tribes. The northern tribes had a number of good leaders and were determined to put up a stiff resistance to anyone who cared to take them on.

That their resistance was stronger then the army's push was demonstrated once gold was discovered in Montana. To protect what came to be called the Bozeman Trail the army foolishly put three forts in the very heart of Sioux territory: they put them up, but soon found that they could not defend them properly from the thrusts of the outraged Sioux. The racist Captain Fetterman, who believed, like Custer, that he could whip all the Indians that were, rode into a Sioux-Cheyenne ambush and found that, in fact, he *couldn't* whip all the Indians that were.

Councils flourished in this period. The Oglala leader Red Cloud, who sometimes kept the negotiators waiting a week or two while he hunted buffalo or otherwise amused himself, informed the government that those forts had to go, and in fact they went—this was in 1868, and was probably the high-water mark for Native American diplomacy. Red Cloud backed the army off, as no one else quite did. The Bozeman Trail remained not safe for miners, but miners came anyway and many of them paid with their lives.

Briefly beaten in the north, the War Department decided to push Kansas as a place they might successfully protect. Railroad workers were busy extending the Kansas Pacific Railroad. They needed to be fed, which is what Buffalo Bill Cody did—and they needed to be protected from raids, which is what, in theory, the army did.

Custer was among the protecting forces. He parked Libbie at Fort Riley, the safest fort, and then proceeded into the great flatness with three hundred men and a band. The latter was thought to improve morale—which, considering the difficulties of the mission, proved a heavy task.

A large—too large—expedition was set loose at about this same time. This was the expedition led by General Winfield Scott Hancock, whose name became a byword for military futility. Thousands of men, loaded down with masses of equipment, really had no chance of catching up with the small, fleet bands of Indians, who easily rode circles around the soldiers. Mobility time and again defeated massive force. General Hancock only bothered the few Indians clumsy enough to stay in range; often the Indians they did locate were not the ones who had completed a raid.

RED CLOUD.

The difficulty of distinguishing guilty Indians from innocent Indians was stated succinctly in a letter from General Sherman to President Grant:

> We cannot discriminate—all look alike and to get the rascals we are forced to include all.

An inability to separate the good from the bad perplexed the army from the first. A famous remark: "The only good Indian I ever saw was a dead Indian," has been attributed to both Sheridan and Sherman. Whichever said it, both probably believed it. Sherman is supposed to have said it to an Indian beggar at the train station in Salt Lake City.

In Kansas, General Hancock didn't close with very many Indians, and neither, for a time, did Custer. The latter was in the clutter and muddle of a miserable trip, which saw his men desert in droves. Evan Connell's figure is five hundred from 1867, and this from Custer's star unit, the 7th Cavalry. That so many chose the desperate remedy of desertion, even in the Kansas flatness where they could be lost, shows how miserable army life could be for those who were not generals.

LITTLE WOLF.

DULL KNIFE.

SPOTTED TAIL.

SITTING BULL.

RED DOG, LITTLE WOUND, RED CLOUD, AMERICAN HORSE, AND RED SHIRT.

BIG CROW WITH THE GUN HE USED IN
THE BATTLE OF THE LITTLE BIGHORN.

ONE BULL WARRIOR.

14

WHILE HANCOCK MAINLY DITHERED, CUSTER marched his troops to exhaustion in pursuit of very elusive foes. He clearly knew that the Hancock expedition was a colossal wash. He did his duty for a while, and then reformulated his duty, left his command, and went in search of his wife.

Libbie Custer had been rather gently raised; she must have been shocked by the coarseness of the frontier. Her books were written many years after the events they describe, and maintained throughout a tolerant and almost bouyant tone.

CUSTER AND LIBBIE AT MEALTIME ON BIG CREEK, KANSAS, 1869.

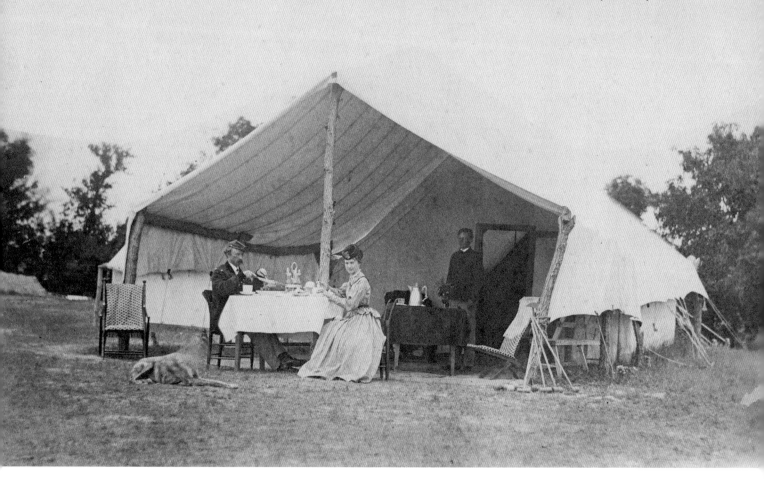

Custer, when he started his search, didn't know where Libbie was. He sent a message urging her to come to him—but then realized that if she obeyed she would be putting herself in considerable danger of capture and the fate worse than death.

While searching he wrote her frequent and lengthy letters, in one of which he pointed out that he was not a monk, a fact Libbie probably knew by then.

Custer apparently rode away from his command with an unfurrowed brow—at least that was the opinion of those who watched him leave—which did not happen until he had enjoyed a good lunch, creature comforts being his natural right. His casual departure from his command was of a piece with his casual execution of guerrillas and deserters.

He found Libbie at Fort Riley and was annoyed, a little later, when the army court-martialed him on eight counts, the most serious charge being abandonment of his command.

He was found guilty on all eight counts and was sentenced to a year's removal from the army without pay. In his autobiography he skirts the court-martial. He went home to Monroe, where he tried his hand at writing articles.

A mere two months passed before General Sheridan began to lobby for Custer's return. Little Phil soon got his way and the Custers moved back to Kansas.

THE BATTLE OF THE WASHITA was fought on November 27, 1868, and was generally thought to be Custer's one great victory in the American West. Its greatness, I suppose, depends on how one grades battles.

It got good press, but at the same time alienated the officer corps of the U.S. Army against Custer permanently; the reason for their hatred and mistrust was the abandonment of Major Joel Elliott and his eighteen men to a cruel fate. Custer could have at least gone and had a look, but he didn't, though Major Elliott and his men were slaughtered just two miles from the main body of soldiers. Their severely mutilated bodies were easily in sight of the main body of troops. Custer later gave his military patron a tour of this then famous battlefield. That no one had attempted to recover the bodies of, after all, American soldiers was another indication, if one were needed, of Custer's callousness. All the men, including Major Elliott, had their penises cut off, that being an old staple of primitive warfare.

The Washita is a small river that runs through the eastern part of the Texas Panhandle and on into what is now Oklahoma. The encampment that Custer attacked belonged to Black Kettle, the famous peace-loving Cheyenne leader. When Custer's soldiers came, Black Kettle managed to get on a horse, with his wife, Medicine Woman, behind him, but bullets soon cut them down. It is said that they lay in the icy river all night but if so they didn't feel the cold. The Washita is little more than a creek.

A fact recorded by some historians but not by others is that Black Kettle and the other Cheyenne were in fact on their assigned reservation. Black Kettle, to the end, tried to play by the white man's rules, although they saw the railroads advancing and their food source, the buffalo, diminishing.

More quickly than anyone would have thought possible the great herds were diminishing. By the time of the Washita battle whole trains full of hunters crossed the prairies. Very quickly where there had been millions there were only remnant herds.

Hunters from Chicago in private cars didn't even bother to step out of the trains: they shot through the windows. Fewer and fewer buffalo were left.

In time the great Comanche leader Quanah Parker, on a visit to New York, bought ten buffalo from the Bronx Zoo and started the Wichita Mountain herd. More recently the mogul Ted Turner has done much to bring the buffalo back to the plains in significant numbers. In large measure, when Black Kettle and his tough wife died, the world they knew died with them.

THE BATTLE OF THE WASHITA.

CUSTER THE MYTH, AS OPPOSED to the man, was the result of two battles: the Washita and the Little Bighorn. Without those two conflicts he would be remembered, if at all, as an inspired young cavalry officer in the Civil War.

His response to both battles reveals his main shortcomings as a fighting leader; most important, perhaps, was his indifference to resonance. Even in his Civil War days he seldom bothered with it, which put his company in peril more than once. In several cases, fortunately, his instincts pulled him through. Like many football coaches Custer firmly believed that the best defense was a good offense.

A considerable dog pack accompanied the 7th Cavalry; once the time had come to attack the Cheyenne encampment these dogs had to be killed, lest their barking alert

CUSTER ATTACKS BLACK KETTLE'S CAMP.

the Cheyenne. Two of Custer's own dogs had to be killed but the stag hound Blucher, who wanted to be Libbie's lapdog, was left at home.

On the Washita as at the Little Bighorn Custer chose to divide his forces. The three groups came to Black Kettle's camp just at dawn. The men waited, cloaked in a dense ground mist; then the morning star shone with unusual brilliance—so brilliant was it that some thought it might be a rocket. (Fireworks were sometimes sold to the Indians by itinerant traders.) The star shone so brightly that Custer, fearing discovery, ordered the charge, and it worked, though this time he wasn't opposed by thousands of Indians.

The band—he always had a band—struck up the popular "Garry Owen," a tune that Custer could never get enough of. The glorious 7th went to work: routing the astonished Cheyenne did not take long. When the fighting ended and the bodies counted there were 103 dead, of which only eleven were full-grown fighting men.

Had Custer had any clear idea as to how many Cheyenne were actually in the area, he probably would have been more prudent. Captured goods were abundant: 573 blankets, for example, and 241 saddles. They took fifty-three captive women, including the lovely Mo-nah-se-tah, of whom more later. The women, the scouts, and the officers were all allowed to choose mounts from the extensive Cheyenne horse herd; when the choices were made the rest of the Cheyenne horse herd was killed, a tactical precaution that Crook used in Montana and Mackenzie used in Texas. The latter killed 1,400 horses in the Palo Duro canyon, effectively ending the Red River War.

Custer had a number of Osage scouts and two white scouts, one named Corbin and a scruffy renegade from California named Joe. The latter favored mules over horses, as did, on occasion, Buffalo Bill Cody. On one occasion Cody guided Custer from one Kansas fort to another and had to put up with much abuse of the mule he was riding, although in the end Custer had to admit that Cody's mule kept up very well with his own thoroughbred.

When Custer brought in his captives and his troops he showed a few threatrical touches himself. He put the Osage scouts first and arranged the captives as if he were conducting a fashion show.

Meanwhile, in another part of Kansas, Hancock made himself even less liked among the tribes by starting a tremendous prairie fire at a depot called Pawnee Fork. A couple of days later three railroad workers were captured and disemboweled, a punishment

Custer parlays with Kiowa Chiefs, Oklahoma.

that crops up frequently in accounts of the brutal conflicts of the time. One woman worker with a baby found herself surrounded; she picked up a knife and with one swoop gutted the baby and plunged the knife into her own heart.

Custer's studied entry into Fort Riley was spoiled by the fact that nearly everybody under his command hated him—the officers in a solid body.

Custer was obliged to toot his own horn after the Washita. Only Sheridan seemed fully pleased, and Sheridan was a sucker for Custer.

Not long after the battle, a piece appeared in the *St. Louis Democrat* criticizing the handling of troops; the piece also mentioned the abandonment of Major Elliott.

In a fury Custer called all his officers together and declared that he would horsewhip the man who wrote the piece. Our old friend Captain Benteen asked to see the text and then frankly admitted that he was the author. He said he was ready to step forward and receive his whipping.

Custer had not expected the culprit to be in the room. It put him in an awkward position and caused him to stammer. He looked embarrassed, as indeed he was, and merely told Benteen that he would see him again.

Indeed, he did see him again, on the morning of the Little Bighorn and lots of times in between.

FREDERICK BENTEEN.

As I MENTIONED EARLIER, ONE of the captives Custer brought to Fort Riley from the Washita was the very comely Cheyenne girl whose name is rendered in various ways, my choice being Mo-nah-se-tah, described by Custer as "being among the aristocracy," certainly an odd choice of words to describe a young native woman. In Cheyenne terms it is hard to say what exactly was aristocratic about the girl. Maybe her husband was rich—he is said to have paid an extraordinary bride price for her, though this would not make her an aristocrat.

Though Custer spoke sloppily here, it is clear that the girl was exceptional. When she tired of her husband she divorced him in a painful way: by shooting him in the kneecap.

This was effective, but it still didn't mean that the Cheyenne had a class system of the sort that suggests aristocracy as we know aristocracy. That she was no one to take lightly is clear—even Libbie Custer knew it. Libbie points out that shooting a husband in the kneecap is a terrible thing to do to a warrior whose status depends on mobility.

Libbie says this in *Following the Guidon*, where she allows herself to reflect on her own complicated feelings toward Mo-nah-se-tah:

> The birth of her baby after her capture, her high position . . . made me anxious to see her, and yet, even when the soft eyes smiled on me, I instantly remembered how they must have flashed in anger when she suddenly drew the pistol from under her blanket and did her husband the greatest injury next to death that can happen to an active warrior. Nor could I help feeling that with a swift movement she would produce a hidden weapon, and, by stabbing the wife of the white chief who had captured her injure him in what she believed would be the most terrible way.

But then Libbie lets herself be disarmed by Mo-nah-se-tah's baby, born shortly after the Cheyenne girl arrived at the fort. That her husband thought so highly of the girl must have irked Libbie at least a little bit. That she consciously half expected the girl to stab her cuts rather too close to the Freudian bone. She may have been eager to admire Mo-nah-se-tah's first baby, but what about her second, born at the fort later in the year. This boy, named Yellow Swallow, may have been fathered by Custer; or not. Nor do we know whether Custer and his brothers visited the dread tent-brothels that sprang up near most army camps. Did Armstrong give Libbie a social disease; and if he did was that the cause of the couple's childlessness? We don't know the answer to any of the questions, and likely never will. Nothing I know suggests that Custer was wildly profligate, though he did some run-of-the-mill philandering from time to time. One can suspect that the months when the childless Libbie had to share Custer with the easily fertile Cheyenne princess were not the happiest of Libbie Custer's life.

Libbie was not at all pleased when the government suddenly decided that the Peace Party might have a point. From planning to kill them all, the government suddenly wanted to go easy on them, at least until the railroads advanced and the buffalo eliminated.

Custer's attack on the Washita drove most of the southern tribes out into the vastness of the Llano Estacado—the Staked Plains. Here, along with the Comach and the Kiowa, they felt unassailable: until Mackenzie assailed them.

Custer, who had just routed them, was told to find them and make peace. It was thought that his words might be more smoothly received if he had some women with him, so he took a few, including Mo-nah-se-tah, with him. Probably he had a fling with this young woman; clearly he liked her very much. What became of her son, Yellow Swallow, is also a mystery. If it had not been for Libbie, Custer might have acknowledged him: there was distinguished precedent for such unions. William Clark, of Lewis and Clark, fathered a son on a Shoshone girl and the boy lived to fight at the Little Bighorn, on the Indian side.

But Yellow Swallow vanishes from the record. In those days that often happened.

Certain aspects of the career of George Armstrong Custer make you wonder about policy with a capital P. Why would they fight one band of Indians one day and then make peace with that same band tomorrow? And why would they send Custer, a lifelong hothead, on a mission that required patient diplomacy? Patience was surely one of the missing elements in Custer's complex character.

Nonetheless, that is exactly what the policymakers did.

Before this, though, was Custer's accidental marriage to Mo-nah-se-tah, which occurred when he placed his hand on her in the Cheyenne camp. It reminds one of Jeffrey Hunter's accidental marriage in *The Searchers*. The ever malicious Benteen says that Custer lived with Mo-nah-se-tah during the winter of 1868–69. If so, where was Libbie?

In any case we know that Custer departed for the Staked Plains with the girl and some Osage and Kaw scouts, his mission being to salvage what could be salvaged with the Cheyenne.

Considering what had just happened the wonder is that Custer wasn't killed. Probably he was chosen for this unpromising mission because Sheridan knew that he had the gall—and the balls—to do it. Custer walked straight into the combined camp of Rock Forehead and Little Robe, both formidable men.

Custer didn't smoke, but allowed a peace pipe to be thrust upon him. He didn't like it but he did it, and the Indians followed suit. When Rock Forehead finished his pipe he deliberately brushed ashes across Custer's boots, a big insult, though it's possible Custer didn't know this; or, perhaps he knew it but accepted it because he knew that the alternative would probably be his death.

Rock Forehead then told Custer that if he ever went against the pipe again he would be killed, and all his men as well.

And so it came to pass in 1876. There are many accounts of the mutilations practiced on some 250 of Custer's soldiers.

RED CLOUD OFFERS A PEACE PIPE AT THE FORT LARAMIE TREATY SIGNING.

LITTLE ROBE.

As all students of Custer know, he himself was not hacked up, though the women of the Sioux and Cheyenne did push their sewing awls through Custer's eardrums. It is thought that this was done because Custer evidently didn't hear Rock Forehead's warning, though he said it very plainly, though not in Custer's language.

When Rock Forehead came into the reservation, Mo-nah-se-tah joined his band, and that was the last anyone heard of her.

AMERICA LIKES HIGHLY VISIBLE COUPLES. The public likes to think that their heroes—whether presidential, military, or even artistic—somehow manage to have admirable, fun marriages, unlike (usually) their own. There's Ike and Mamie, Jackie and Jack, LBJ and Lady Bird, Pat and Dick, and, of course, Nancy and Ron. And I've already mentioned Jesse Benton Frémont, whose role in her husband's life was enormous.

Libbie Custer, somewhat in the same mold, was probably the leading professional woman of her time. She tirelessly took up the cudgels against her husband's many critics.

Supporters of Major Reno were particularly likely to draw down a tirade from Libbie.

Defending the man was one thing, actually living with him quite another. The 1860s ended. The Custers were always highly social. Since they were stationed mainly at Fort Leavenworth, St. Louis was a handy place to get away, where usually they stayed at the Southern Hotel, where one day Libbie snapped; she unloaded on Armstrong, leaving a mass of criticisms on his head. Custer would never forget her "distressing words." In time he would respond, in a letter quoted by Shirley Leckie in her excellent biography of Libbie. By this time the Custers had been married about six years—they were at the halfway point. In attempting to answer Libbie's attacks he brings up his own feelings, noting, to begin with, an absence of fervor—that fervor and that joy. He makes his laments, mentioning that her lovemaking had become mechanical, depriving him of the warmth he had become dependent upon.

Then he voices the fear that Libbie will never love him again as she had, though "while I am absent you may think kindly of me and remember much that is good in me, but when I return the spark of distrust which I alone have placed in your mind will be rekindled and little burning words will be the result." He goes on to say that his love for her is unquenchable, as unquenchable as his life.

We are long accustomed to thinking of Custer entirely in military terms; it requires a shift in focus to think of the hero Long Hair coming to grips with the fact that his wife is slipping away. He probably cheated on Libbie, and he constantly broke promises, but he did seem to love her and he clearly did not want to lose her.

Frederick Benteen, critical as ever, said that Libbie was the coldest woman he ever knew; since he thought Custer was also cold the couple may have been in that respect well mated.

Marriages are notoriously opaque—it is hard to know exactly when Libbie began to distance herself from George. By the 1870s it was observed by many that the couple mostly traveled alone, rather than—as had once been the case—together.

Officially the vice that most distressed Libbie about George was his gambling. He was very fond of faro, and, like most compulsive gamblers, really needed the risk.

Maybe he fought for the same reason: the risk.

Gambling, of course, took him into low company, which may have been what Libbie hated most about her husband's vice. She knew her husband well enough to know that he would not be likely to put up much resistance to some advance from some beauty of the demimonde.

Army posts in Kansas and elsewhere were notoriously plain and usually deadly boring. Flirting was one of the few admissible diversions. Libbie herself made a decision not to flirt, but she could not find it in her heart to criticize those who did.

The Custers, when the 1870s started, were neither more or less happy than most couples in their position. They socialized a lot and traveled when opportunity came their way. After their years on the plains they finally got a quiet posting in Kentucky, close to the racetrack: something for Armstrong to bet on.

All parties, though, knew that the 1870s were merely the calm before the storm. And not even very calm—the Red River War came in the early 1870s and the finale in the middle of the decade.

The buffalo were now being slaughtered by the millions; Custer went back to the plains for a celebrity hunt now and then.

In the councils of the Sioux and the other plains tribes there was dark foreboding. The whites were crossing in ever greater numbers. Red Cloud made his treaty and the three forts vanished from the Bozeman Trail. But General Sherman's view slowly prevailed: the red man must be killed or securely confined. The general himself was lucky—twice lucky in fact: the first time was in Texas, when the Kiowa could have had him had they been paying closer attention: he passed right in front of a war party that, later in the day, massacred seven teamsters. The second lucky escape was in the newly established Yellowstone Park. He was picnicking with his family and was nearly swept up in the famous retreat of the fighting Nez Perce. Sherman thought the Indians were putting on a show for himself and his family, when in fact they were busily murdering Montanans.

LIBBIE CUSTER, 1862.

LIBBIE IN HER WEDDING DRESS, 1864.

GEORGE AND LIBBIE.

GEORGE AND LIBBIE, 1865

CUSTER AND LIBBIE RELAXING WITH FRIENDS.

THE KANSAS PLAIN IN THE 1870s was probably more popular with sporting people and the curious rich than it has ever been since. That was mainly because of the surge of railroads and the distinctive comfort of the private car—the Learjets of their day. Tycoons, newspapermen, and, on rare occasions, even royalty seemed compelled to shoot the large, stupid American bison. Hunting them brought a little color into the lives of the many soldiers who had to find something to do in places that might fairly be described as raw.

Undoubtedly the most important visitor during the 1870s was the Grand Duke Alexis of Russia, third son of Czar Alexander II. The Grand Duke was tall, like his father, but he was myopic, and far from being the sharpest knife in the Romanov drawer. Though his main interest was in chorus girls or their equivalent, he liked a little sightseeing—the Kentucky-based Custers showed him Mammoth Cave—he did especially want to shoot a buffalo.

A group was soon formed to assist the monarch's hunt. The Custers were part of it, but the real hero of the royalty hunt was Buffalo Bill Cody himself, who in his years as a showman became quite comfortable with royalty, including (this came later) Queen Victoria. Cody not only put the Grand Duke in reach of the buffalo, he also, at some risk to himself, went into the country of the Brulé Sioux and persuaded their leader, Spotted Tail, to bring his warriors and do a little war dancing for the visitor. Spotted Tail (Crazy Horse's uncle) was not loath to put on a show for the whites if the presents were generous, as they were in the case of the Romanov's visit.

The Grand Duke's shooting was so erratic that there was some danger to the horse herd; Cody may actually have shot the buffalo the Grand Duke thought he killed. Nine buffalo were killed in all, some probably with an assist from the very experienced Cody.

Elizabeth Custer was there too. In fact the Grand Duke liked the Custers so much that he invited them to New Orleans with him. They accepted and a good time was had by all. It was probably better than sitting around watching the fissures in their marriage widen.

CUSTER WITH GRAND DUKE ALEXIS OF RUSSIA.

Quiet, shady Elizabethtown, Kentucky, might have seemed an ideal place for the Custers to settle down and repair their frayed relationship; but it didn't work out that way. For couples deep in the marital stews no place is likely to prove ideal. Both Custers read a great deal; it was one way for couples to ignore one another.

Lexington, Kentucky, was home to America's version of the sport of kings. Custer, of course, seized every opportunity to get out to the races. He was irked that his beloved 7th Cavalry was in the south, fighting the Ku Klux Klan and generally helping out with Reconstruction. It was to come back to him a little later on.

Libbie observed that a good many of her fellow army wives were beginning to eat too much and get fat—she took more care with her diet but eventually she grew plump anyway. By that time though she was the famous Widow Custer.

In Washington to seek a livelier post, Custer twice tried to see President Grant, but Grant, who had no patience with Custer, managed to elude him.

When relief finally came for Custer it was because the Northern Pacific Railroad was pushing into Indian country near the Yellowstone and was often under attack, the attackers mostly being the Sioux. Custer was finally summoned to the Dakotas, working out of Fort Abraham Lincoln, across the river from Bismarck.

To his chagrin, Custer was not put in charge of this caretaker expedition. This plum went to General David Stanley, who disliked Custer about as much as Custer disliked him. Custer's innocent cookstove was the cause of many quarrels. Custer wouldn't give it up and Stanley couldn't stand it.

When the Custers arrived, in 1873, Custer immediately went hunting and killed an antelope whose blood unfortunately dripped on some doughnuts he had been saving for Libbie. Could this be an omen? Could the comet that showed up later in the year be an omen? Custer himself was not superstitious; the comet was probably just a comet.

Custer was aware, as was General Stanley, that the surveying party was treading pretty close to prohibited land: in particular the Black Hills, Paha Sapa, holy to the Sioux.

CUSTER'S HOME AT FORT ABRAHAM LINCOLN, NORTH DAKOTA.

In 1868 the army, aware of its own weakness—there were those burned forts—made a treaty giving the Black Hills to the Sioux in perpetuity, which meant forever.

There had been, by this time, several hints about gold in the Black Hills; at first these were tentative hints, not enough to spark a full-scale gold rush, something that certainly would come if the gold appeared to exist in commercial quantities—as in time it did.

The Northern Pacific was punched through without serious battle. Custer amused himself by catching small animals that he sent to the New York zoo. He caught a porcupine and a wildcat, both of which were soon traveling eastward. An elk tore up several dogs. The elk was dispatched and Custer made a stab at learning taxidermy, an elk being a lot of animal to practice on.

It may be that, for a time, Custer wavered about the Black Hills. He knew that if there was gold there, there would be a war for it. Should he let the Sioux keep their holy place, or should he discover the gold himself, becoming overnight a national hero?

If in his depths he aspired to be president, a likely time for this aspiration to surface would be 1874, when Custer was at last able to lead his own expedition into Paha Sapa.

CUSTER IN HIS STUDY.

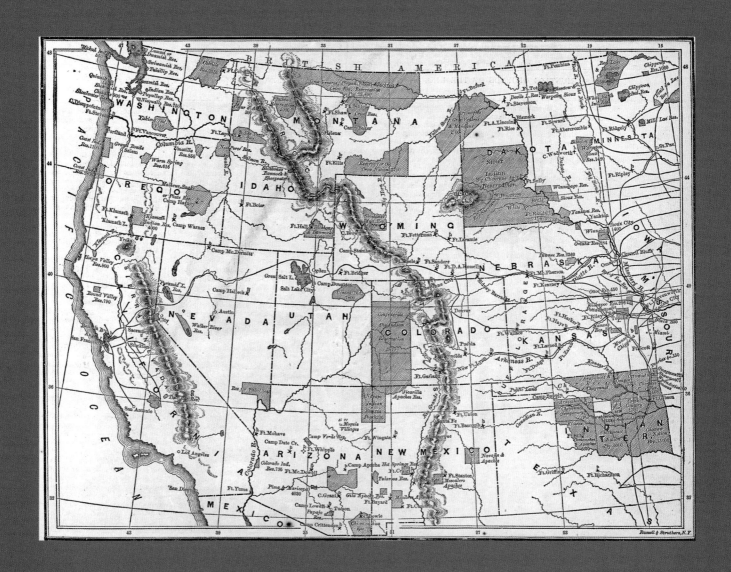

THE 1868 TREATY GIVING THE Sioux the Black Hills was known to people who wanted to repeal it merely as "That Pact." The public clearly had the right to Black Hills gold, if there was any. At least it was felt that there *should* be a second expedition, to find out the truth about the gold. This was the famous 1874 expedition, commanded, to his great delight, by General George Armstrong Custer.

In case anybody doubted that they were coming they took along a sixteen-piece band. Just before he departed from Fort Abraham Lincoln the General posted a long letter to the *New York World* in which he had this to say:

> We are goading the Indians to madness by invading their hallowed grounds, and throwing open to them the avenues to a terrible revenge, whose costs would far outweigh any scientific or political benefit possible to be extracted from it under the most favorable circumstances.

But then this perverse man proceeded to lead just such an expedition; and he did find substantial evidence of just what the expedition had been looking for in the first place. It wasn't visible in the roots of the grass, as Custer had casually predicted, but the gold *was* there, and, in the next few decades, millions of dollars' worth of it would be mined. Custer went, with no loss of sleep, from being a responsible prophet to being in essence the area's first real estate broker.

There would be many more.

Custer's next consideration was how to announce this news. He didn't really need to emphasize his own contribution, since he was already thought of as the man who found the gold.

Laramie, where there was the nearest telegraph line, was nearly one hundred miles away, and there were many hostiles between Custer and the telegraph line. In the end he entrusted this important news to Lonesome Charley Reynolds, his most reliable scout.

CUSTER'S WAGON TRAIN EN ROUTE TO THE BLACK HILLS.

CAMP AT HIDDEN WOOD CREEK.

CUSTER'S BLACK HILLS EXPEDITION WITH FRED GRANT, 1874.

Lonesome Charley prudently traveled at night, taking four days for the trip. He carried a canvas mailbag with these words tacked on:

Black Hills Express

Charley Reynolds Manager

Connecting with all points East, West, North, South

Quick rates; quick transit

We are protected by the 7th Cavalry

IN THE BLACK HILLS.

Well, protected for the next two years, maybe. Lonesome Charley should have realized that he could not really afford the careless Custer, whom he died with at the Little Bighorn.

Once he heard of Custer's coup, Grant quickly called his military men in. It was obvious that the treaty of 1868 was now so much wastepaper: the rush to the Black Hills was now unstoppable, unless the Indians stopped it by killing so many miners that the whites gave up—this was very unlikely, although the Indians did kill a great many.

A FAR-SEEING CONSIDERATION—THAT FUTURE LEGALITIES might eventually favor the red man—prompted the government to eventually try to simply buy back the Black Hills. There was yet another conference, but Crazy Horse spiked it immediately by sending an emissary to say that he would kill anybody who sold even an acre of the Black Hills. The emissary was Little Big Man, the same who would hold Crazy Horse's arms as he was being bayoneted in Fort Robinson. The Little Big Man of Thomas Berger's novel was someone else.

This sale did not proceed. A second effort in 1876 ended inconclusively. At the time the Battle of the Little Bighorn occurred the status of the Black Hills was very much in dispute.

The American masters and commanders were ruthless men. Grant, Sheridan, Sherman, and the rest had seen Shiloh, Vicksburg, Gettysburg, and the Wilderness. All had witnessed great carnage, but they were sensitive to the fact that solemnly making a treaty and reneging on it five years later smacked of dishonorable behavior.

Grant and his friends eventually adopted a see-no-evil speak-no-evil policy which essentially ignored the problem of the treaty. The public debate was extensive, and somewhat one-sided: most Americans emphatically favored taking back the Black Hills and digging out that gold. And if the Sioux didn't like it, they could lump it.

Only a few foresaw the day when the Sioux would be educated people who could hire pricy lawyers to represent them.

Clarity, if not justice, was attained the next year, when the whites simply took back those famous hills.

As I mentioned earlier, the journalist Alex Shoumatoff reckoned that the United States had made 354 treaties and broken them all. It is possible to see the whole continent, from Point Barrow to the Golden Gate, as one big land grab. Wavering over the Black Hills and then taking them is the type of process that had occurred many times—always with the same result.

Throughout 1875 travel by whites in the Black Hills was an extremely chancy thing. The government took a hands-off policy: anyone who wanted to head into those hills was taking a big chance, but the discoveries at first were rich enough to keep the miners coming. The extralegal process by which we took back the Black Hills was clearly a disgrace.

Tales of miners coming in with coffeepots full of gold were mostly false but still widely publicized.

Custer went home to Libbie a national hero again. What Libbie felt about it is not known. In any case he wasn't home for long.

My partner, Diana Ossana, and I were given a blessing ceremony in which we were brushed with the three eagle feathers the great Comanche Quanah Parker carried when he brought his people onto the reservation in 1875. We were conscious of having received a great honor.

Ranald Mackenzie himself met a sad fate. One night before he was to be married to a Texas lady, he got into a saloon brawl, was soundly beaten and left outside all night, tied to a wagon wheel. In fact he went insane that night and never recovered. His bride-to-be never recovered either. That great cavalry officer who defeated Dull Knife's Cheyenne in 1877 was never to regain his sanity; he lived out his life in an asylum.

RANALD MACKENZIE.

Evan Connell says that Kit Carson led Mackenzie to the Palo Duro, but this is a rare mistake. Kit Carson died in 1868, a month after the death of his beloved wife, Josefina. Kit did participate in the First Battle of Adobe Walls. His commander, James Carleton, ordered Kit to clean out the Indians surrounding the old trading post, but when Carson arrived he found too many Indians and only escaped by firing the grass.

The Indians called Mackenzie Bad Hand and they respected him far above most white soldiers. After all he fought them in *their* place and no one else had done that.

As an officer Mackenzie was similar to Custer. Both thought little of defying expected behavior. Mackenzie was far more stoical than Custer. The latter loved creature comforts. Mackenzie was so indifferent to comfort that his men sometimes draped blankets over him to keep him from freezing in bitter weather, of which there was no shortage.

Mackenzie, with no written order, took his troops across the Rio Grande to rout the Lipan Apaches, who were raiding from what they thought was a secure base. His victory over Dull Knife of the Cheyenne, in the winter of 1876, was the one significant victory in the confused and clumsy efforts to punish the tribes that wiped out Custer and his men. The night of the attack was so cold that eleven Cheyenne babies froze; the Indians were shocked that the whites would fight in such weather. The soldiers, following the example of both Crook and Custer, destroyed all the provender in the village, not even having the foresight to save some of the abundant buffalo meat for themselves.

Custer surely knew, as he approached his death, that there were a *lot* of Indians ahead of him. But the dust the horses raised would have prevented him from realizing that the combined encampment stretched some four miles. In no encounter during his life on the plains would he have seen even a tenth this many Indians.

He did realize, suddenly, that he was in trouble. He scribbled a note to Benteen, which he handed to the Italian trumpeter John Martini, whose English was not trustworthy:

Come on, be quick. Be quick.
Bring packs.

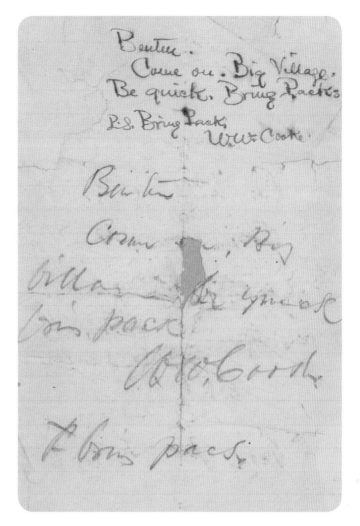

CUSTER'S LAST MESSAGE.

Historians consider it to be a note missent: Benteen had nothing to do with the pack animals: those were under the command of officer Thomas McDougall.

Custer, realizing that he was in real trouble, may not have been thinking too clearly. The note survives, and is now in the library at West Point.

The vigor with which the U.S. Army pressed the Red River War, against not very many savages and in mostly inhospitable climes, suggests that the government was at last ready to play the endgame, finally and thoroughly. But they didn't really do it effectively. The biggest battle—Custer's—was won by the eventual losing side.

If one takes a literary rather than a historical view of the great battle one might suggest that the Battle of the Little Bighorn is the point at which the narrative of American settlement ends.

That the settlement had been successful was never seriously questioned again, not as the Indians contested it that hot day, June 25, 1876, by a little river slicing through the rolling plains of southern Montana. The army chased Indians around the plains for another two years with few serious confrontations. Mackenzie had already whipped the Comanches in the Palo Duro Canyon. In Arizona both Crook and Miles had some trouble with the Apaches, but when Geronimo finally came in he had only eighteen warriors with him, a few more than Custer slew on the Washita. Geronimo might make a life in the mountains of Mexico, as he did for a time, but he was never going to win his war.

Whether one starts in the far northeast with Cabot, or in Virginia with John Smith, or in Mexico with Cortéz and Coronado, the natives, over and over again, are invaded and eventually lose their culture.

The wonder is that this one reversal—the Little Bighorn—in which the ultimate losers win, is so rare. It nearly happened to Lewis and Clark when they were braced by the Teton Sioux near the Mandan villages. Fortunately the captains had a cannon and were prepared to use it.

This provides an odd link to Custer, who, famously, was offered Gatling guns, but passed on them because he knew they would slow him down.

There is a huge amount of native prophecy about the arrival of these white people. Even as early as the sixteenth century native preachers were preaching about the destruction of the whites and the return to the paradise that had been theirs before they came.

Then the Little Bighorn happened and the Indians killed the arch-invader, and so ends the American settlement narrative, with dying men and horses on a dusty plain, a place far different from the places most Americans were by then living their lives.

A complex justice evolved on that battlefield, a justice that, years later, was still being debated. Custer's comeuppance became America's comeuppance, for three centuries of shabby treatment of the red man, the taking of the Black Hills being merely the latest and most striking example. Custer's defeat was the nation's defeat, and, ironically, the Indians' defeat as well. For three centuries the Indians had mattered. They had a secure place in the American narrative.

And then they didn't. It was very strange. Something was over, but neither the Indians nor the whites knew what.

People mourned, and yet could not say quite what they mourned.

So intense was the publicity following the Little Bighorn that when the famous gunfighter Wild Bill Hickok was shot down in Deadwood, South Dakota, the nation, usually attentive to gunfighters, scarcely noticed.

GENERAL CUSTER'S EXPEDITION ON THE MARCH.

CUSTER'S EXPEDITION ON THE MARCH.

In the late 1970s, not quite one hundred years after the battle, I was in Montana working on a movie eventually called *Montana*; it wasn't made until fifteen years after I wrote my drafts. I stayed in Lame Deer, the northern Cheyenne headquarters town, for two weeks. The movie was about the opposition to strip mining, but the time I spent in Montana was not so much preparation for writing a movie as it was for writing this book.

Lame Deer, where I spent two weeks, was not as bad a place as Pine Ridge, but it was bad enough. The main street was filled with rusted cars. It was bleak, but I decided to stay there rather than in the hard-bitten town of Hardin, Montana, a town notoriously cruel to Indians.

Eventually I switched to a motel near the battlefield. It was grim, but so was everything else in Montana.

In Hardin there are not one but two annual reenactments of the Battle of the Little Bighorn, one put on by the town itself and the other by the powerful Real Bird family. I did not see either one. I then lived in Virginia, where reenactments of Civil War battles were a kind of plague. I did, over the years, visit a few of the major battlefields, discovering in the process that I was not really a battlefield buff.

In Montana I noticed that the guides to the battlefield were all Crow. The Crow scouted *for* Custer, and have been pretty much the white man's Indians ever since. In Montana neighboring tribes—Crow and Cheyenne—could not be more different. In two weeks on the Cheyenne reservations I had maybe two conversations. In one day on the Crow reservation I had at least a dozen.

The Cheyenne fought Custer, for which they were exiled to the Wind River, the reservation that has had the greatest number of teen suicides among Native Americans. Some were taken as far as Oklahoma. In 1878 about three hundred Cheyenne fought their way out of the dreaded Oklahoma reservation and made for their Montana home. The revolt was lead by Little Wolf and Dull Knife. Theirs was a heroic march; most

Custer battle reenactment.

were cornered in Nebraska, but a few did make it. Though hotly pursued, some admiration was felt for the heroism of the march, which can be seen in the John Ford movie *Cheyenne Autumn*.

I was privileged to hear the story of the Cheyenne Long March from the mouth of a Cheyenne elder, Mrs. Elk Shoulders. At the time I didn't know what I was hearing, but a translation arrived in a few days, and I enjoyed it. I didn't enjoy Mrs. Elk Shoulders so much because her emphatic Cheyenne made it seem that she was angry with me.

The surviving Cheyenne were put on a reservation near the Tongue River, where some of them are today.

There is a small park in Lame Deer, and a plaque marks the spot that the survivors returned to. My cowboy hero, early Montana rancher Teddy Blue Abbott, thought the Cheyenne march a tremendous thing. Their resistance was astonishing.

Once I thought about it I realized why the Cheyenne of Lame Deer didn't want to talk to me. Why would they? The Cheyenne of Lame Deer were part of the bad, punitive legacy of Custer. The older Cheyenne don't want to assimilate, and some of the young Cheyenne sided with them, against their parents, most of whom now wanted the white man's goods, if not the white man's way.

Being in Lame Deer was a painful experience. The Crow had long ago sold their coal to the strip miners; the Cheyenne refused, and hired a team of Harvard lawyers to argue that pure, coal-dust-free air was essential to their religion. So far the Cheyenne are winning. The big coal-fired station in Colstrip was, for a time, the only one actually built in Montana.

The Crow are not so much venal as future-minded. I went with my son James to their sun dance and there were so many white anthropologists there that the event might as well have been held in Harvard Yard.

The bitter scorn of the Cheyenne is harder to forget than the Crow sun dance or anything else I saw in Montana.

THOUSANDS AND THOUSANDS OF COMMENTS have been made about the Battle of the
Little Bighorn in the more than 130 years since it was fought. In the years just after
the battle very few of these comments were made by Native Americans. This was self-
protection. Some Indians who fought in the battle held their tongues for forty or fifty
years—but once the Indians ceased to be afraid they would be punished, the testimony
came in a flood. And, across three or four generations, it is still coming.

I am not, I repeat, a battlefield buff, and I am not even sure I should call myself a
historian. I walked the Custer battlefield twice, without, I confess, being very moved by
what can now be seen. I was more interested in what the Crow guides were telling the

LITTLE BIGHORN RIVER, 1886.

LITTLE BIG HORN RIVER,
WEST SIDE RENO CROSSING,
CUSTER BATTLE FIELD.
JUNE 25th 1886.

tourists. Had there been Cheyenne guides the tourists would have been told a different story.

If you seek details about the battle itself, I would refer you to Evan Connell, Robert Otley, James Donovan, and Nathaniel Philbrick, who, between them, sweep in virtually everything verifiable about the battle, as well as a few things that are pure guesswork. Read these four books and you can consider yourself very well informed about Custer, his men, the Indians, and the battle itself.

As to the battle itself, historians now think that as many as ten thousand Indians, mainly Sioux and Cheyenne, were camped along Little Bighorn creek, in a generally north–south axis. Perhaps a quarter of these were warriors, the rest women and children.

Major Marcus Reno, on Custer's orders, with his three companies, attacked this huge gathering of Native Americans from the south; he soon realized he was catastrophically overmatched and fled back across the river with what men he could, to seek the protection of the nearby bluff, where he dug in and held out.

Custer, well to the northeast, did *not* know of Reno's routing. He, confident as ever, charged down into the valley of the Little Bighorn expecting to put the sav-

ages to flight. Some think he made a desperate attempt to turn north, only to be blocked by Crazy Horse, but that may be romance. In fact he and his men were all very soon dead. Custer was hit twice.

What I would like to convey here is something of the atmosphere, the ambience that existed on the northern plains when Custer and the other generals, Terry and Gibbon, marched off from Fort Lincoln to subdue the Sioux.

I would also like to consider some of the enduring mysteries the conflict engendered, hoping to see them in the context of the times. I would like to sketch in an overall view of the battle as we now know it.

MAJOR MARCUS RENO.

There was a plan, approved by Grant; Terry and Gibbon tried to follow it and did follow it, only to discover when they got themselves and their large body of troops to the mouth of the Bighorn River that Custer, the rebel general, had simply ignored the order and marched his men somewhere else, to the mouth of the *Little* Bighorn River, some distance from where they were.

Why this surprised anyone I don't know: it was just the kind of thing Custer would be sure to do. He was the child-man who never learned to share and, on this occasion, had no intention of sharing. As Custer was riding out of Fort Abraham Lincoln, Terry called after him, asking him not to be greedy, to save some for them. Custer answered with a wave and went determinedly on his way.

Throughout his career Custer had never been known to wait for anyone. In part this was his perpetual restlessness, his own need for glory. In part though it was a miscalculation about the Indians; he was convinced that the Indians would always run if faced with well-disciplined, well-generaled soldiers. This was probably based solely on his victory at the Washita, where he only killed eleven warriors because most of the other Cheyenne who were there saw running as their best chance.

Custer, though, rarely reasoned from his own experience. At the Little Bighorn he ignored all tradition and put his soldiers into battle at midday, when they were very tired. Had the assault been made at dawn the Indians might have missed the fatigue— as it was they saw the soldiers' legs wobbling. Seeing how dead tired the soldiers were must have raised the confidence of the Indians a good deal. Crook's men had not been tired a week earlier, at the great Battle of the Rosebud, and yet the Indians won. Now there were many more Indians and the soldiers were tired at the *beginning* of the battle; by the time it ended they were not tired: they were dead, as was their commander.

George Crook, the most experienced Indian fighter the army had (with the possible exception of Mackenzie), always claimed victory at the Rosebud, but no one agreed with him, and his claim was made halfheartedly.

Crook had been ordered to sweep the Powder River, where he found few Indians. Then, on the Rosebud, one week before the Battle of the Little Bighorn, he found plenty; but for the bravery of his Crow and Shoshone scouts, he might have suffered a very costly defeat—the Rosebud rankled him all the rest of his life. In his readable autobiography he argued that he won, but most students of the battle think otherwise.

In Crook's favor is the high death toll of the Indians: thirty Indian dead at least; Crazy Horse, who was there, counts thirty-six, which would be an enormous loss for a hunter-gatherer people. Crook's loss was eight, and yet Crook was good. Had he not been good the death toll among the whites would surely have been much higher.

Most of those warriors who survived the Rosebud were there at the Little Bighorn. Sitting Bull, though, was not at the Rosebud.

Immediately after the Battle of the Rosebud, General Crook retreated one hundred miles south. The retreat may represent his real conclusions about that difficult battle. What puzzled Crook were the huge numbers of Indians buzzing around that part of the country. He had not expected to find Indians in such numbers. Realizing that there

LONESOME CHARLEY REYNOLDS.

might be even more nearby, he immediately dispatched a courier to Fort Abraham Lincoln, warning Custer, Terry, and Gibbon not to take the Indians lightly. This did not arrive until all three generals had left, and did not catch up with them until it was too late.

These couriers, like Lonesome Charley Reynolds, had to cross hundreds of miles of country teeming with hostile natives. Like Lonesome Charley, they chose to travel mostly at night.

The question that has most disturbed or engaged historians ever since is whether Custer, had he had the warning from the south, would have behaved more prudently. Most historians doubt that he would have. I agree. Whatever he and Crook thought of one another, it is unlikely that Crook's troubles would have swayed Custer at all.

SIOUX PREPARING FOR THE BATTLE OF THE LITTLE BIGHORN.

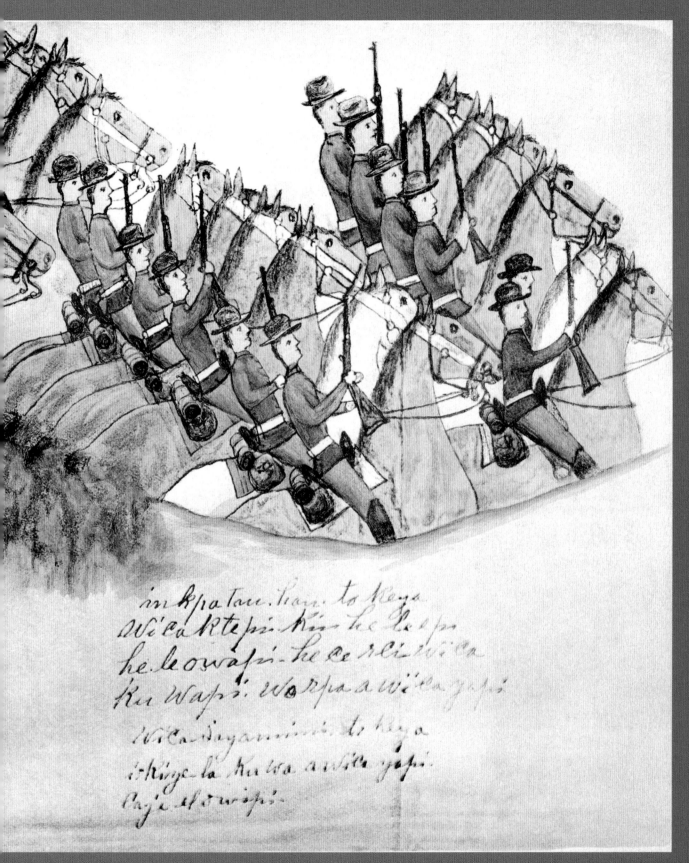

OPENING OF BATTLE OF LITTLE BIGHORN BY AMOS BAD HEART BUFFALO.

CUSTER'S LAST CHARGE.

W. Herbert Dunton

SIOUX INDIANS FIGHTING AT THE LITTLE BIGHORN.

CUSTER'S LAST RALLY.

Frederic Remington

THE SOLE SURVIVOR.

EVERYONE IN A POSITION TO advise Custer, as he approached the Little Bighorn, concurred on one precaution: he should not divide his force. Keep it *one* force. Sensible advisers listened to the many scouts, who were certain that Indians in numbers long unseen would be met with on the Little Bighorn. For more than a week scouts had been reading sign and exchanging information, None of the scouts had ever seen so many trails. To this day historians argue about how many Indians Custer faced. The upper number might be ten thousand, with a quarter of those warriors and the rest women and children. No one in living memory of Indians had seen a fighting force that large. Even the few elders who remembered the Laramie conference didn't think it had been *that* large.

Custer, if he even heard these numbers mentioned, probably considered them gross exaggerations. Many military men might have disbelieved the figure. Hunter-gatherers could not afford to spend much time in groups that large. Where would the food come from? Mention ten thousand Indians in a group and many frontiersmen would shake their heads in doubt.

But the conflict at the Little Bighorn turned out to be one of those occasions when received wisdom was wrong.

Custer, in any case, had made a career of defying received wisdom. He said to someone that he could beat 1,500 red rascals. Probably never for a moment did he expect more.

Could he have won, had he kept his troop together? He had, all told, about 670 men. Would that number have been enough to back these Indians off? We'll never know, but on paper it looks a lot better than 250, which is about what he personally went to war with.

Major Reno, the villain of the story in Libbie Custer's eyes, had three companies, Benteen had three companies, and Custer had five. And more were with the pack train. And, in fact, Custer may only have faced about 1,500 men; the other thousands may not have existed.

When Custer addressed that final note to Benteen he can have had no real idea where Benteen was: he had sent him to check out some badlands. Custer was within an hour of his death by then; he may have admitted to some miscalculation—to himself, at least. So he tells the distant Benteen to be quick, when Benteen is probably in no position to be quick. And then it all falls apart.

What did he feel as it fell: dismay, terror, confusion, determination? There's a legend that when he fired his last bullet he smiled or laughed. Although who could have seen this last smile is not clear. Many of the Indians would not know of Custer—it is hard to know, or in fact impossible to know. Nathaniel Philbrick has a good chapter on the smile, which we only know about because Private Thomas Coleman, who found the body, mentions it. Custer's final smile is one of the true mysteries of the Little Bighorn.

In time several Indians claimed to have killed Custer. Which one did we don't know, but we do know that he was shot twice.

CUSTER WAS RASH—ALL HIS LIFE, rash. He was, for most of his life, an extremely confident man. He trusted his instincts to see him through, and, in the Civil War years particularly, they did sustain him. When he divided his troops he did it almost casually. He ignored Benteen, an experienced man, and he ignored the rest of his officers as well. "Custer knows best" was his unspoken motto.

Excellent reconnaisance was available to him but he ignored it as well. Custer just did not want to be bothered. What he wanted was to get on with the fight.

All Custer's native advisers, without exception, told him that he would die if he went down into the valley of the Little Bighorn.

What surprises the reader, or this reader at any rate, was that the scouts themselves expected to die, and did, one being Mitch Bouyer, a half-breed said to be the protégé of the famous mountain man Jim Bridger. He could speak English. Custer's favorite scout, Bloody Knife, also expected the worst. Bloody Knife was standing near Major Reno when he caught a bullet in the head; Major Reno was splattered with Bloody Knife's brain matter. Many historians think that this gruesome circumstance unnerved Reno—it would unnerve most people. Reno had seen plenty of carnage during the Civil War but being splattered with brains might indeed have had a bad effect, one not to be overlooked—but it probably should not be exaggerated, either. He did not behave unreasonably once the battle was joined.

To a man the scouts said the whites would die if they rode into the valley; then, to a man, the scouts died with their military leaders. They did not flee, although most would probably have escaped had they done so. Was there then a scouts ethic: you must rise or fall with your commander.

It seems to me that the role of native scouts in the conquering of the Indians has been understudied. Buffalo Bill Cody was a fair scout himself. Crook gave full credit to his Pawnee scouts, who found him the hostiles he was looking for. And the Red River explorer, Captain Randolph Marcy, had a Delaware scout named Black Beaver, who was

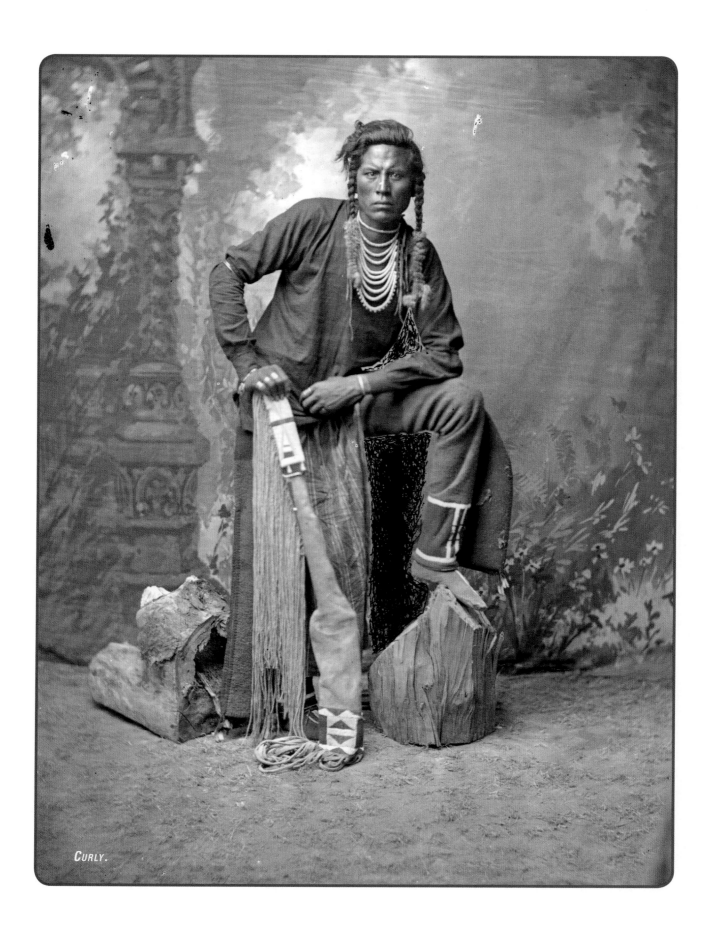

CURLY.

THE FAR WEST.

said to know every creek between the Columbia River gorge and the Rio Grande. Kit Carson could have made the same claim.

Crook's Crow and Shoshone scouts saved his bacon at the Rosebud. The gunman Tom Horn was one of the few white scouts who gained the respect of the Apaches he helped locate. Later, he became a gun for hire, killed a young boy, and was hung.

On the subject of survivors, the great Hunkpapa Gall, a man so impressive that he even impressed Elizabeth Custer, had only scorn for Curly, the scout who was the one escapee from the Little Bighorn. Mitch Bouyer told Curly to get, while there was still time, and Curly got. He was the one who brought the news of Custer's defeat to the waiting crew of the steamer *Far West,* who didn't believe him at first. Later, when Curly advertised himself as the one survivor of the famous battle, Gall was withering in his scorn. Where are your wings? he asked, for once the Indians had Custer surrounded only a bird could have gotten out.

No one who saw Gall ever forgot him. He had been injured nine times, several times seriously, and yet he rose from death again and again. Libbie Custer put it this way:

> Painful as it is for me to look upon the pictured face of an Indian, I never in my life dreamed that there could be, in all the tribes, so fine a warrior as Gall.

Custer, Scout Bloody, Private Noonan, and Captain William.

Mitch Bouyer.

vise Custer to keep the troop together, to which advice Custer merely said, "You have your orders."

Evan Connell suggests politely that Custer may have fallen victim to West Point military emphasis, which it took from European theory, which argues for attack. The French particularly believed in attacking the head of the opposing forces. Kill the head, the theory was, and the body dies.

Still, while this may be some bit of an explanation, everybody who advised Custer before the battle insisted that he had no plan at all. To be aggressive: that was his plan. If he had any other plan he surely kept it in his head. He was always, as a general, wholly confident of his ability to improvise.

The terrible result can be seen at the Little Bighorn Monument. Students of mutilation, if they could have arrived when the battlefield was fresh, would have had much to

LITTER FOR THE WOUNDED.

Libbie Custer believed, and argued publicly for about five decades after her husband's death, that if Reno had sustained a proper charge the Indians would have turned tail and run. She believed what her husband always believed, which was that faced with a well-trained modern army *all* Indians would run.

Reno himself got tired of having his judgment questioned endlessly in the press; after a while he demanded—and got—a court of inquiry. This was held in Chicago, in the Palmer House, and resulted in an official endorsement of what Reno had done. Officer after officer testified that if Reno had not turned back when he did—if he had gone even three hundred yards farther into the camp—he and all his men would have been slaughtered.

Libbie Custer was bitter—she continued all her life to argue that her husband could have been saved and the Indians defeated if Marcus Reno had only pressed his charge.

Nobody now believes Libbie. The testimony of the Indians themselves, once time had passed and the fear of punishment diminished, bore out Reno's judgment: he had wisely turned back at the last possible moment, thereby saving most of his men.

Custer, who was sampling two fine kegs of liquor from one of the packs, probably had no idea that Reno was as deep in trouble as he had been.

Reno had crossed the river to make his charge, and recrossed it under hot pursuit in order to save what he could of his command. Once back across the river he got on a small bluff, with some vegetation to provide cover, and there he stayed until the Indians stopped bothering him, and left. His command was joined by most of Benteen's troop, who also fought for their lives.

Benteen blamed the Italian trumpeter Martini for circulating the "Hurrah boys, we've got them" remark. Benteen called Martini thickheaded, among other choice names. Benteen was probably the last person to ad-

JOHN MARTINI.

As I HAVE SAID, MAJOR Marcus Reno proved to be the principal antihero of the Battle of the Little Bighorn. Custer had given Reno orders more precise than those he gave Benteen—the latter also survived, with most of his men. Major Reno's orders were to ride south to the foot of the big village, and then charge through it, pursuing the Indians who, it was presumed, would be in flight. Custer thus burdened Reno with his own deeply flawed analysis of the mission they were engaged in. Neither Reno nor Custer had any real sense of the size of the encampment they were attacking. Reno woke up only when he noticed that a solid wall of Indians were charging *him*, which was definitely not the way the attack was supposed to happen.

ONE DEPICTION OF RENO'S RETREAT.

CROW ARMY SCOUT FOR CUSTER.

BLOODY KNIFE, CUSTER'S SCOUT.

CUSTER WITH CURLY AND HIS DOGS.

After the battle the Indians waited to see if there would be an immediate response. None came; late on the second day after the battle the Indians decided to leave. It was feared that, by then, many white soldiers might be coming to the Little Bighorn, to avenge Long Hair.

Only a few white scouts happened to see this great exodus. To them it seemed that the prairie had become a moving carpet of people, with travois, thousands of horses, dogs, babies, and the people themselves, many of them subdued. Most went south at first, though some angled off to the northwest. Neither Terry or Gibbon laid a finger on them—though that calm would not prevail for long. The whites, Sitting Bull knew, were a determined people. They would be coming.

The whites, indeed, did come, but in the short run ended up with very little to show. At first they put their strength in numbers: Crook had two thousand men, an absurdly cumbersome troop, and Terry had nearly that many, about 1,600. In a way it was the Hancock expedition all over again. The Indians stayed mobile and easily eluded these armies. Their only real slipup was Mackenzie's raid, that freezing night, on Dull Knife's camp. Otherwise there were mainly small skirmishes: a few dead here, a few dead there. Slim Buttes, where the first little skirmish was fought, had only a handful of lodges, not enough to satisfy a public howling for revenge. The public wanted the Indian to be struck a terrible blow, but this didn't happen.

One encounter that at least made good copy was Buffalo Bill Cody's taking of the famous "First Scalp for Custer." Cody, at the time pursuing a career on the stage, was way over in the Carolinas when Custer fell, but not for nothing was he a showman. He quickly got himself west and was sent to serve under General Wesley Merritt's command, then operating near Fort Robinson, in Nebraska—the fort where Crazy Horse was killed. General Merritt was trying to get as many Indians as possible to go into the Red Cloud agency, where they could be peaceably processed.

On his first morning in camp Cody put on one of his velvet suits—later it was ru-

Oakley chose to treat it comically: she was, after all, married for more than fifty years. Sitting Bull was a man who enjoyed some success with white women—a lady philanthropist from Brooklyn had stayed in his lodge for a while, just before he was killed. Whether their relationship was platonic and philanthropic is also a matter of debate. Robert Utley believes that in fact there was some kind of romance there. The poor Brooklyn woman's son died of lockjaw while she was in the Dakotas. Improbable romances did sometimes occur when savages and do-gooders got together.

The best Sitting Bull could offer in his pursuit of Annie was many cattle, more than she would have had any use for. He called her his Little Sure Shot and remained her biggest fan. She did let him know that she appreciated his devotion.

A day or two before Sitting Bull was shot dead by a Sioux policeman he claimed to have heard a meadowlark speaking to him in Sioux, something that, in his opinion, the cheeky bird had no business doing.

When the terminal gun battle broke out at Sitting Bull's home, the old warhorse that Buffalo Bill had given him after his one season on the Wild West Show began to go through his paces—unhappily his owner would never be in the saddle again.

As for Sitting Bull at the Little Bighorn, how much influence he might actually have had over the ten thousand natives there is not easy to estimate: let the reader decide. Perhaps by then he felt that he had really fought enough.

The whites, he knew by then, would fight on forever, or until they attained their end.

The Indian way was different.

by his spiritual efforts during the week before it, when he first had a medicine man cut one hundred small pieces of flesh from his body.

Then he danced—on and on he danced, while looking up at the sun. Finally, still dancing, he fainted; and when he came to, he had his famous vision of soldiers falling into camp. The soldiers, as rendered by a native pictographic artist, seem rather like grasshoppers.

When he was a boy, Sitting Bull was thought to be slow. His first name, in fact, was Slow. But, in a battle fought when he was nine, he he counted coup, which made for immediate promotion name-wise: he got his father's name, a common thing among the Sioux. A similar thing happened to Crazy Horse, who also got his father's name; his father was then called Worm.

How much influence Sitting Bull actually had is a matter for debate among historians. Robert Utley has written a fine biography called *The Lance and the Shield*, which lays out various arguments about the man that Buffalo Bill, in a famous understatement, called "peevish." He had intense eyes and he hated white people. With the two exceptions I noted earlier: Buffalo Bill Cody and Annie Oakley, whom he frequently tried to marry.

During the battle itself, Sitting Bull is said to have exercised his influence by advising *against* digging out Major Reno and his men from their position on the bluff. The Indians could easily have dug them out and annihilated them with all the rest, but they held off. One theory is that Sitting Bull gave this advice—if he did—because he knew how extremely vindictive the whites were likely to be. Killing Custer would produce revenge enough, which it did. After the battle General Miles hassled Sitting Bull's band particularly. Sitting Bull finally got enough of being chased all over the plains; he took his people to Canada, which did not work out very well. They nearly starved, although the Canadian government offered some help.

When Sitting Bull arrived at the Canadian border he showed the officials a commemorative medal that had been given to leaders who came to the Laramie conference in 1851. Such medals are very rare now. I once found one in London, on Portobello Road.

Sitting Bull's passion for Annie Oakley was real, if a little comical—at least Annie

THE X-FACTOR IN THE BATTLE of the Little Bighorn was the surly Hunkpapa known as Sitting Bull, a warrior and a medicine man. Several commentators suggest that Sitting Bull exercised more political power with the Indians than any Indian leader of his time.

He is thought not to have fought in the battle itself, but he prepared the way for it

SITTING BULL.

MONROE COMMERCIAL.

VOLUME 36. MONROE, MICH., THURSDAY, JULY 13, 1876. NUMBER 28.

THE COMMERCIAL.

Published every Thursday, at No. 19 Washington Street, MONROE, MICH., by
M. D. HAMILTON & SON,

TERMS OF SUBSCRIPTION.—$2,00 per year, free of postage. A discount of 50 cents for advance payment.

ADVERTISING.—Transient advertising, one square (10 lines), one week, $1.00; two weeks, $1.50; three weeks, $2.00; four weeks, $2.50; and 25 cents for each insertion thereafter.
Liberal terms to yearly advertisers.
Local business notices, 15 cents per line.

JOB PRINTING.—Ample facilities for all kinds of Plain and Ornamental work. Prices low and satisfaction guaranteed.

CITY BREVITIES.

Hot weather the past week. See weather report.

C. G. Johnson, Esq., left for the Centennial, day before yesterday.

The Eagle Hose Co. will give a steamboat excursion to Sandusky in the latter part of August.

A good healthy summer drink is the root beer made by T. B. Case, of Lasalle, and cheap too. Mr. Case comes in town two or three times a week, to supply customers.

Last Saturday evening about 9 o'clock, a very bright meteor lighted up the sky, moving over our city in a northwesterly direction. Its track through the sky could be seen for 20 or 30 minutes.

Sackett's show window, contains the portraits of Gen. Custer, Thomas and Boston Custer, and Armstrong Reed, draped in mourning and surrounded by a profusion of American colors.

The old friends in this city, of Miss Emma Smith, some years ago a teacher in our Union School, and who for several years past has been a resident of California, will find her marriage recorded in this paper.

David Reed Esq., left last Friday evening for Fort Abraham Lincoln, with a view to ascertain what can be done about obtaining the bodies of Gen. Custer, and the group of his relatives who died with him, and also to accompany home the sorrowing women at Fort Lincoln.

The interior of the M. E. Church has been handsomely draped in mourning, in memory of the fallen Custer and his comrads. A bas relief portrait of Gen. Custer, properly draped, occupies a conspicuous position on the organ, fronting the audience, and surrounding it, within wreaths of evergreen, appear the names of his four relatives who died by his side. Last Sabbath Rev. Mr. Casler preached a discourse appropriate to the occasion (though not a funeral discourse), from the text in Revelations "Be thou faithful unto death, and I will give thee a crown of life."

Casualties.

On the 5th inst, a son of Louis Eckert, ten years of age, while playing on a wagon loaded with bags of grain, fell off and was run over by the hind wheel, dislocating the left elbow joint and otherwise injuring him. He is recovering.

On the 7th inst, a son of Edward Roeder, three years of age, got his hand caught in the cog-wheel of a clothes-wringer. Result—one finger off. A rather severe initiation into the trials of this life.

On the same date, a man in the employ of Mr. Robert G. Kelly of Erie, Fred Springer by name, aged about 20 years, was thrown from a mowing machine, and falling upon the knife-bar, had his right thigh badly lacerated, with a fracture of the bone. The limb was amputated by Dr. Southworth, assisted by Drs. Gifford and Thompson of Erie. The man rallied somewhat after the operation but it is doubtless a fatal case, as at 5 P. M. full reaction had not been established.

☞ Killed in an attack made upon the Sioux Indians, in Montana, June 25th, 1876, Gen. Geo. A. Custer, Col. Thomas Custer, Lieut. Calhoun, Boston Custer, and Armstrong Reed.

At a meeting held at the Monroe M. E. Church, July 6th, the following resolutions were adopted:

Whereas, The above named have fallen gallantly fighting the foes of our common country, and,

Whereas, So many of the near relatives of the deceased are members of this church, therefore,

Resolved, That we deem it fitting that some formal action be taken, by which as a church we may recognize the high esteem in which these men were held among us, and our admiration for their valor. That as soon as possible we may fix on a suitable time, a memorial shall be held in this church. That the church be draped for thirty days in honor of the fallen heroes. That we extend our tenderest sympathies to the families of the deceased. That a copy of these resolutions be sent to each of the bereaved families, and to the press of this city for publication.

D. CASLER,
O. A. CRITCHETT, } Committee.
J. M. LOOSE,

Weather Report.

The following shows the state of the weather for the week ending yesterday.

	7 a. m.	2 p.m.	9 p m.	Max.	Min.
Thurs., July 6	69 ab.	88 ab.	82 ab.	92 ab.	67 ab.
Friday, " 7	73 ab.	93 ab.	84 ab.	[illegible]	[illegible]
Sat., " 8	79 ab.	95 ab.	86 ab.	99 ab.	71 ab.
Sunday, " 9	79 ab.	99 ab.	87 ab.	101ab.	75 ab.
Mon., " 10	78 ab.	93 ab.	77 ab.	96 ab.	76 ab.
Tues., " 11	70 ab.	89 ab.	83 ab	91 ab.	69 ab.
Wed., " 12	[illegible]	[illegible]	[illegible]	[illegible]	[illegible]

CUSTER FALLEN!

TRIBUTE TO HIS MEMORY!

Our City in Mourning!

PUBLIC MEETING AT THE COURT HOUSE!

BUSINESS CLOSED!

Speeches, Resolutions, &c., &c.

The news which reached this city last Thursday morning, of the death of the heroic Custer and his brave comrads is confirmed in all its fulness and terrible extent. As soon as our citizens fully realized the calamity that had befallen them—that had befallen our State and our country at large, a gloom settled upon every heart, like a pall. For Custer belonged to his country; Michigan honored him and gloried in his military career; and here at Monroe, in the home of his school days and young manhood, kindred and friends have watched his career with loving pride. They have known him as a brave, manly, heroic, chivalrous spirit, true as steel in every trial, and they have believed him worthy of higher honors than those the government has seen fit to bestow upon him. But he is now no more! All hearts are filled with sorrow; all heads are bowed in grief. We weep not alone for a friend and brother, true and good, but we weep also for a fallen brave—a friend and brother whose place in our hearts can never be filled—a fallen brave whose place among the braves of the nation no other brave can supply. Our warmest sympathies go out in hearty spontaniety to his young wife and his sister, both bereft of their companions and left alone afar off on the frontier; and most especially are our sympathies extended to his aged parents, who not only lose him, but also two other sons and a son-in-law, all brave and true; and we should not forget the parents of the younger relative, the only son of our townsman David Reed, who was in his first battle and died by the side of his heroic uncle. For the dispatches say, "the bodies of Custer, his two brothers and nephew (with several other officers) were found lying in a circle of a few yards." They had made an attack, were apparently compelled to retreat, were cut off from the man body, forced into a narrow recess, where horses and men were slaughtered promiscuous—two brothers and nephew (with several to tell the tale.

On Friday morning last by order of Mayor Spalding, bills were circulated calling a public meeting at the Court House at 4 o'clock the same afternoon, at which time business was closed—business houses had previously been draped in mourning. At four o'clock the bells were tolled, the band marched to the Court House playing a dirge, and the building was soon filled with our sympathetic and mourning populace. The Hall had been appropriately draped in mourning, and a portrait of Gen. Custer, properly draped, was arranged just back of the speakers stand.

The meeting was called to order by Mayor Spalding, who made some remarks proper to the occasion, appropriately styling Gen. Custer "the Murat of the U. S. Army."

Mayor Spalding was made chairman of the meeting, and John M. Bulkley was named as Secretary.

Rev. D. Casler offered a prayer befitting the occasion.

Mayor Spalding read a dispatch from Vice President T. W. Ferry under date of Washington, July 6th, closing as follows: "I share the grief of Gen. Custer's home in the fall of this cavalry hero. He fell as he fought—in the fore front of battle. The country will miss this brave soldier, and friends cherish his gallant memory." Also a dispatch from W. H. Walby, H. Hart and other citizens of Adrian as follows: "Adrian mourns with you on the news of the death of the gallant and chivalrous Custer and his brave comrads. We deeply condole with his amiable wife and other friends in their great bereavement."

On motion of Col. Grosvenor, a committee was appointed to draft resolutions to be presented to the meeting, said committee consisting of Col. I. R. Grosvenor, E. J. Boyd, R. E. Phinney, G. M. Landon, and E. C. Harvey.

Remarks were made by W. H. Boyd, Rev. Dr. Strong, J. D. Ronan, Frank Raleigh, J. M. Bulkley, and E. J. Boyd, each paying a fitting tribute of respect to the deceased, and of sympathy with the afflicted parents and other relatives.

R. E. Phinney, from the Committee, read the resolutions, as follows:

WHEREAS, By a Providence which only the firmest faith in the wisdom of Him who sits as the dispenser of all events, can justify, our city has been stricken with profoundest grief at the seemingly untimely death of so many of her young men, noblest in heart and life, fullest of future promise,

Resolved, That we friends and acquaintances of those who have so ruthlessly been taken from us, find most grateful comfort in the memories they have left us of their chivalric spirits and noble achievements; that in the death of Gen. Custer, to the wife of that knightly soldier, Calhoun; to the parents of the brave, pure minded boy who fell on his first field of battle, and to the whole circle of their kindred we tender our heartfelt sympathy and condolence; reminding them as we remind ourselves, that henceforth these fallen ones are no longer ours, nor theirs, but our country's and fame's, among the pure, the immortal names that are not born to die.

The resolutions were adopted, and on motion the secretary was directed to furnish a copy to the parents of the deceased.

A committee consisting of E. J. Boyd, J. M. Sterling, I. R. Grosvenor and J. M. Bulkley, was appointed to send a dispatch of condolence to Mrs. Custer and Mrs. Calhoun, at Fort Abraham Lincoln.

After another dirge by the band, the meeting was closed with prayer by Rev. D. P. Putnam. The bells were tolled during the exercises.

BIOGRAPHICAL.

Gen. George Armstrong Custer was born at New Rumley, Harrison Co., O., about 20 miles from Steubenville, on Dec. 5th, 1839. In 1852 he came to Monroe to reside with his brother-in-law, David Reed, and attended school here several years. He always after called Monroe his home. After returning to Ohio he spent a year or two in teaching, and in 1856, while Congressman John A. Bingham of that State, was canvassing his district, young Custer jocosely told him he would vote for him if he (Bingham) would send him to West Point; which Mr. Bingham promised to do if he should be elected, and he was as good as his word. Custer entered West Point in 1857. From his early youth young Custer had a great desire for military life, his ardent wish being to become a soldier. Soon after he entered West Point his parents moved to Monroe, and his vacations were always spent here. He left West Point in July 1861, went to Washington, and was immediately sent to the front with dispatches to General McDowell, and was assigned to duty just in time to participate in the first battle of Bull Run. From that time forward through the war he followed the fortunes of the Army of the Potomac, participating in nearly every battle. He rose from rank to rank, and in 1863 was brevetted Major General of Volunteers, and was afterward assigned to the command of the Third Cavalry Division. During the last six months of the war, this cavalry division, under General Custer's command, captured 111 pieces of artillery, 65 battle flags, and over 10,000 prisoners. They never lost a gun of art color, and were [illegible] After the war Custer served a short time in Texas, and then joined Hancock's expedition against the Indians, since when he has been in constant service on the frontier, and by his bravery and prowess made himself a terror to the red men. In 1864 he was married in Monroe to the only daughter of the late Hon. Daniel S. Bacon, who was born and had grown to a lovely and accomplished womanhood here in this city of flowers, among the friends who now mourn with her the fall of her adored hero. After their marriage his wife was with him always at his headquarters on the frontier, and accompanied him on many of his expeditions in the field. Since the war Gen. Custer has been improving a portion of his time in the arena of literature, and with marked success. His book entitled "My Life on the Plains," which first appeared in successive articles in the Galaxy, is a very entertaining book, containing much information relating to Indian life and warfare. He spent the most of last winter in New York, revising and preparing for publication his "War Memoirs," the first two or three chapters of which have been published in the Galaxy, the remainder of the series being completed and in the hands of that journal, for publication. The last number of the Galaxy contained a graphic sketch by Custer entitled "Battling with the Sioux on the Yellowstone."

Thomas Custer entered the army in 1862, as a private, and participated in Gen. Sherman's grand march to the sea. In the volunteer service he rose to the rank of Lieutenant-Colonel, by brevet. After the war he was transferred to his brother's cavalry command in the regular army, and has been with the General in most, if not all of his campaigns against the Indians. He ranked as Captain in the regular army.

Boston Custer, another brother of the General's, was in the commissary department. He has been with his brother's command several years.

Lieutenant James Calhoun, brother-in-law to the General, is the son of a widowed mother living in the State of Indiana. He was highly esteemed by all who knew him here in Monroe.

Harry Armstrong Reed, Gen. Custer's nephew, was the only son of David Reed, Esq., of this city. He was born in Monroe, was 18 years old in April last, and was known and esteemed as a very promising young man. He, with his sister Emma, left this city with the General in May last, accompanying him to Fort Abraham Lincoln. "Autie," as he was called, accompanied the expedition as a herder. His parents have a letter from him dated June 10th, and written in camp on Powder River, 20 miles from its junction with the Yellowstone, in which he speaks of Custer's command as about starting to find Indians, and said

THE REGATTA!

The Champions of the World in Monroe!

And their Names are Sho-wae-cae-mette!

The Floral City Club Captures the Four Oared Junior Prizes!

A CLEAN SWEEP FOR MONROE!

The eighth annual regatta of the North Western Amateur Rowing Association, held in Toledo on the 4th, 5th and 6th, was by far the finest regatta ever held by the association, and equaled, if not surpassed, any regatta ever held in the East. A large concourse of people witnessed the races each day, and the promptness with which the races came off showed that the officers were faithfully performing their duty.

The principal race of the first day was the four oared free for all, in which there were four entries, the Wah-Wah-Sums, of Saginaw; the Cincinnatis, of Cincinnati; the Puritans, of Toledo, and the Sho-wae-cae-mettes, of Monroe. The Puritans having only entered to further the success of the regatta, and with no hopes of winning the race, did not pull over the course but laid for the Sho-waes at the mile stake, coming in a half length behind. At the start the Wah-Wahs took the lead with the Cincinnatis next, until breaking an outrigger the latter fell behind. At the mile buoy the Sho-waes were some ways ahead. Here the Wah-Wahs, mistaking the buoy, lost considerable time in attempting to turn, but as soon as the Sho-waes discovered what they were at they informed them of their mistake and the race continued, the Sho-wae-cae-mettes winning in 18:25 with the Wah-Wah-Sums full twenty lengths behind. The following are the crews:

"CHAS. G. MORRIS," Sho-wae-cae-mette Boat Club, Monroe—Crew: Stroke, Stephen Dusseau, 160; Joseph Nadeau, 183; Moses Nadeau, 130; bow, Geo. W. Bowlsby, 135. Total 563 lbs.; average, 140¾ lbs.

"SARAH A. BULLOCK," Wah-Wah-Sum Boat Club, Saginaw—Crew: Bow, Jas. Jerome, 150; John Kellerin, 165; Henry Smith, 165; stroke, P. Manning, 165 Total, 645 lbs.; average 161¼ lbs.

"CINCINNATI," Cincinnati Rowing Club Boat Club, Saginaw—Crew: Bow, Jas. Total, 645 lbs.; average 161¼ lbs. Keenan, 142; J. P. Numan, 135; Wm. Steinheim, 160; Henry Kalish, 140. Total 592 lbs.; average 148 2 3.

The time made in the above race was a surprise to everybody but Monroe people, as it was generally believed that no such time could be made. When the Wah-Wah-Sums passed through the city on their way to Toledo they were told that Sho-wae-cae-mettes had rowed 3 miles with a turn in 18:22, but they would not believe it and went over to Toledo confident of winning both the free for all four, and the senior four. But their hopes of remaining the champions of the North Western Amateur Rowing Association for another year were much diminished when they learned the time made in the free for all; for they frankly admitted that they never had made any such time and did not expect to.

A heavy gale on the second day prevented the races from being called at the appointed time, and the senior four did not come off till about seven in the evening. The water was rough, and it was thought by many that the Cincinnatis and Wah-Wah-Sums had the advantage on that account, but, though they may have had the advantage, it was not great enough to win them the race, as the result proved. The *Blade* says the "race for senior four oared shells was the one in which the greatest interest was manifested, for in this the Wah Wah-Sums, who sustained such a bad defeat the day before at the hands of the Sho-wae-cae-mettes, hoped to retrieve their fallen fortunes, and show the boys from Monroe, as well as boating men in general, that the old Saginaw, though once defeated, was still alive, and its crew could yet pull a boat without looking over their shoulders to see all the rest of the boats. Then the Cincinnati crew, dissatisfied with their showing on Tuesday, when, by accident to their outrigger they were thrown out, determined to make another effort to carry back a prize to the Ohio river. The Sho-wae-cae-mettes said nothing, but trusting not so much to their skill as oarsmen as to their great strength and endurance, determined that they would convince the Saginaw boys that their previous victory was not the result of an accident, but the fruit of good hard work." That the Sho-wae-cae-mettes should say nothing and the *Blade* man be so well informed, is a mystery still unexplained. The positions of the crews were Cincinnatis first, or nearest the grand stand, Wah-Wah-Sums second, and Sho-wae-cae-mettes third. At the start the Cincinnatis shot ahead, pulling a short sharp stroke, with the Saginaws second, pulling their customary long sweeping stroke. It was soon evident that the race was between Saginaw and Monroe, and at the end of the first mile the Wah-Wahs and Sho-waes were nearly even, winning the race by at least four boat lengths, in 18:30¼. The *Blade* says the Sho-waes did not "pull well together but managed to push their boat through the water at a rapid pace." While we deny the statement that they did not pull well together, we are perfectly willing to admit that they did "*manage*" to push their boat through the water at a pace rapid enough to beat the best time on record just six and two-fifth seconds, and on the second day, when the water was very rough at the lower end of the course, they "*managed*" to beat the best time on record (made in smooth water two years ago) a little over one second. Last year Toledo papers laid their success in the junior four to "beef" and a "grindstone" stroke. This year it is their enormous strength and endurance which they trusted in (and which enabled them to win), rather than in skill, which Toledo seems unwilling to grant them. The Sho-wae-cae-mettes handled their shell in the most dextrous and skillful manner, shooting in any direction with the velocity of an arrow; and when the boat went over the course in the race, the perfect bee line which the boat took from home stake to turning stake and from turning stake to home stake was the wonder of all who understand boating matters. The *Blade* says they did not pull together, but there never was a more erronous statement than that, as each oar worked with the precision of clock work, the spoons all striking the water at the same time as though one oar. There certainly is a peculiarity in their rowing, that to the inexperienced eye, would seem perhaps as though they were not pulling together, but whether it was through ignorance on the part of the *Blade* reporter, or unwillingness to tell the truth, we are unable to determine. Certain it is that the Toledo papers have ever been willing to slight Monroe in any particular, and still more certain have they seemed unwilling to give a fair account of the races in which she has been personally interested. Why they should be so, when it is for the interest of Toledo to remain on friendly terms with the Monroe boat clubs, is more than we can imagine. However, such good time was made in the four oared and six oared races, that the association determined to challenge all amateur clubs in America to row at the next regatta to be held in Toledo next summer. A "grindstone" stroke, "strength and endurance," "beef," and the "giant" proportions of the stroke, who weighs just five pounds less than any man in the Wah-Wah-Sums crew except bow, (while the average of the Sho-waes is 20½ lbs. lighter than theirs) have done all this. What will they not do to row at the next regatta to be held in teach them the stroke they call "skill." If the Toledo *Commercial* reporter, who is the cause of the one thousand and one mistakes that occur in that paper's report of the regatta is the one who made such a mess of it last year and then came over to Monroe and attempted to make amends by giving a miserably mixed up account of the River Raisin Navy regatta, we would advise the *Commercial* to shove a frog down his throat and tell him "go dwell with them, in some remote region where thy voice can be heard no more on earth."

The next race in which Monroe took part was the four oared junior race on the sixth. The following are the crews, taking their positions in the order named:

"FRANK H HURD," Floral City Boat Club, Monroe—Crew: Stroke, Charles Hoyt, 138; James F. Grant, 150; Geo. S. Willits, 144; bow, Walter P. Sterling, 119. Total 551 lbs.; average 137¾.

"H. B. TAYLOR," Undine Boat Club, Toledo—Crew: Stroke, C. P. Thomas, 155; L. W. Hunter, 155; A. J. Kaeisser, 160; bow, J. W. Hepbourn, 142. Total 612 lbs.; average 153 lbs.

"KENILWORTH," Farragut Boat Club, Chicago—Crew: Bow, Chas. S. Downs, 135; Frank Booth, 145; Henry P. Smith, 135; stroke, A. Ogden Downs, 145. Total 560 lbs.; average 140 lbs.

"GEO. E. HALL," Excelsior Boat Club, Detroit—Crew: Stroke, C. D. Waterman; J. E. Watson, H. E. Hass; bow, John B. Malony.

The Amateurs were entered for this race, but withdrew on account of the sickness of their stroke.

At the start the Farraguts shot ahead, but after the fifth stroke the Floral Citys were ahead and maintained the lead to the last. At the end of the first mile the Undines were close to the Florals, the Farraguts next and the Excelsiors away in the rear, when the latter gave up and returned. At the turning stake the stroke of the Undines, who were close to the Florals, broke the button off his oar, rendering it useless, and leaving the race to be contested between the Farraguts and Florals, the latter winning in 20:22.

The badges won by the Monroe clubs at Toledo this year are very beautiful as well as valuable, the twelve badges costing just $700. Those won by the Sho-wae-cae-mettes in the open to all, are by far the most valuable and we believe are considered the finest badges ever presented by the association. Each badge consists of three massive pieces. The upper piece or bar, to which the pin is attached is of Roman gold, surrounded by a raised border of polished gold with a design of vines at the bottom. In the center of this piece are engraved the words "Open to All" in plain block letters. The second piece, or badge proper, description gives no idea of the beauty and richness of these badges which can only be seen to be admired.

The badges of the senior four consist of a plain bar with place for engraving the name of winner and time made in the race. Hanging from this is a design of four oars, the handles of which are fastened together at the bottom with a rope of gold, tied in a sailors knot, which describes a circle, winding about the blade of each oar, and holding them in a fan shaped position. In the center of the circle described by the rope, and lying upon the handles of the oars, is a streamer of red enamel on which in gilt letters are the words "Senior 4 Oared, Toledo, Ohio, 1876." These badges are valued at $50 each.

The badges of the junior four, though costing but half the money, are much prettier, in our estimation, than those of the senior four. The bar is plain, with a place for engraving time and name of winner. Hanging from the bar by a chain is a beautiful design of crossed oars and a twisted wreath; the blades of the oars are fastened to gether by a gold cord, from each end of which hangs a tassel. Upon the face of the badge, in the shape of a letter S, is a banner of blue enamel on which are inscribed in gilt the words "Junior 4 Oared, Toledo, 1876" in plain gothic letters.

The above badges can be seen in the window of L. & J. F. Grant's jewelry store.

The following is a list of the winners of each race during regatta:

Single sculls—open to all—Frank E. Yates, 140; Union Springs, N. Y. Time 14:27. Prize, gold badge, $100.

Pleasure boats—open to citizens of Toledo—"Zip"—J. G. Kaney, W. G. Alexander. Time 19:20.

Four oared shells—open to all—Sho-wae-cae-mettes—Monroe. Time 18:25. Prize gold badges, $400.

Junior double sculls—"Lotus," Farragut B. C.—Chicago—Bow, A. Ogden Downs, 145; stroke, C. S. Downs, 135. Time, 15:42 4-5. Prizes, gold badges, $50.

Senior four oared shells—Sho-wae-cae-mettes—Time, 18:30¼. Prizes gold badges, $200.

Junior six oared shells—"Wm. A. Halleck," Zephyr B. C., Detroit. Crew: Stroke, E. Barrows, 138; P. W. Keating, 145; C. H. Dings, 143; David Linn, 138; Edward Sutton, 145; bow, Frank S. Bagg, 126. Total, 835 lbs.; average 139 1-6 lbs. Time, 19:15½. Prizes, gold badges, $150.

Barges—"F. G. Thompson," Phoenix B. C., Detroit. Crew: Stroke, C. Creedan: D. Creedan, P. McGrath, M. Schaffer, A. S. Martin, O. A. Jasnowski, J. Byrns, Capt. Creedan, C. Clinton; bow, W. T. Schaffer; captain, Henry Hopkins, 135. Time 13:12½. Prizes gold oars, $50.

Junior single sculls—"Perhaps," H. M. Butler, 120; Chicago scullers. Time, 15:56. Prize, gold badge, $35.

Senior double sculls—F. E. Yates, Grand Haven; Oscar Aeday, Cincinnati. Time, 14:11. Prizes, gold badges $100.

Junior four oared shells—Floral Citys, Monroe — Time 20.22. Prizes, gold badges, $100.

Senior single sculls—"Elsie," F. W. Montgomery, Chicago scullers. Time, 16:20½. Prize, gold badge, $75.

Senior six oared shells—Wah-Wah Sums, Saginaw, Crew: Bow, James Jerome, 150; V. B. Paine, 158; B. McElgann, 158; John Kelorin, 165; Henry Smith, 165; stroke, P. Manning, 165. Total 953 lbs.; average 156 5 6. Time, 17:28. Prizes, gold badges, $300.

A Monument to Gen. Custer.

Ed. Commercial.—Believing it will meet the views of many military and civilian friends of the late Gen. Custer in Monroe and throughout the land, I would suggest that a meeting be held immediately for the purpose of taking steps to secure donations from citizens here and Gen. Custer's friends wherever they may reside, in this or other States, to erect a suitable monument in our Public Square, to him who has so greatly distinguished his own name and left so glorious an example for the young men of our common country.

I would name Col. Grosvernor, Gen. Spalding, R. E. Phinney, Harry A. Conant, John M. Bulkley and John R. Rauch, to take the matter in charge and call a meeting at such time and place as they may select,

Respectfully,
CHAS. G. JOHNSON.

Heartily concurring in the suggestions contained in a communication of our townsman, Hon. C. G. Johnson, relative to the propriety of adopting some measure by the citizens of Monroe for the erection of a suitable monument to the memory of their late distinguished fallen citizen, General G. A. Custer, unite in calling a meeting to be held on Thursday evening, July 13th, in the Court House Square, for this object.

T E Wing,	W H Boyd,
Harry A Conant,	W A Noble,
J M Bulkley,	J A Loranger,
J P Hogarth,	E Vanderheyden,
S M Sackett,	Leonard Mitchell,
C B Stoddard,	L Berthelote,
L Grant,	James L Robert,
W Stoddard,	F Soleau,
M D Hamilton,	E C Harvey
J F Grant,	L R Little,
Darius Loose,	James Little,

Monroe Mourns.

weren't, on the high plains. And yet the cultures have been dying a slow death, ever since. The Indians became prisoners, where they had once roamed free. But by the time Custer was upon them they had nothing to lose from an all-out fight.

When the other, noncombatant Indians found out about Long Hair's defeat it was with a mixture of grief and fear. The fact that they had won a great victory made the Indians happy only briefly—they knew that in winning they had finally lost.

How information about the Little Bighorn and the terrible wipeout of Custer traveled is a mystery. Only an hour or two after the battle had ended, General Crook began to notice that his native scouts began to look sad, wailing and generally expressing a sense of calamity. But what did they know, and how did they come to know it?

This question has never really been answered, to my satisfaction or anyone's. The natives mourned something they could not have seen, and knew something they could not have come to know by conventional means or methods.

General Crook worried this question for the rest of his life, without ever coming to a satisfactory conclusion. Could it have been smoke signals, or hand mirrors, or what? Crook went to his grave not knowing.

At first, everywhere, so improbable was Custer's defeat that it could not be accepted. As I've said, Curly, the survivor, could not at first convince the crew of the *Far West* that Custer was dead.

To a degree the whole nation had the same problem. The shock was similar to the shock of 9/11, in that the whole nation felt it. Surely it couldn't have happened. Those two great buildings could not have fallen. Similarly, George Armstrong Custer could not have let some Indians whip him. It couldn't be—and yet, improbably, it was. The news across the northern plains was generally treated as an insult of some sort. How dare they, these uppity savages?

Not surprisingly, the foreign press was not very sympathetic. *The Times* of London led the way, pointing out that our long history of relations with the Indians had never been either wise or kind.

No journalist in America dared to be that blunt.

mored that the Indians liked his suit better than they liked his fighting, but, be that as it may, Cody loped off, observed by two soldiers with telescopes, who were supposed to keep him from getting into trouble—no easy job with Buffalo Bill. There was an abundance of Cheyenne to the north, and one warrior decided to attack Cody—or he may have hoped to bag two couriers on their way from the fort.

In the reported version of this event, and in the movie version, in which Jeff Chandler played Cody, the two hurled insults at one another, but if so neither of them was in earshot and neither of them could speak the other's language. All the dialogue between them in various books and movies is wholly bogus.

BUFFALO BILL SCALPS YELLOW HAIR.

What wasn't bogus was that the encounter was deadly, and Cody—despite having his horse step in a hole and go down—did kill the Cheyenne, who was named Yellow Hair, not Yellow Hand, as has sometimes been said.

Cody did scalp the dead Yellow Hair and did hold up the first scalp for Custer—it turned out to be one of only a few. Cody may not have been a scout of the first rank, but he had done a fair amount of real scouting and he was well aware that lots of Cheyenne would soon be coming down upon him.

The scalp itself followed a curious path. Cody sent it to his wife, Lulu, in Rochester, New York. The two were on the outs at the time. They mainly were on the outs, following an initial period of bliss.

BUFFALO BILL CODY.

Buffalo Bill, by his own admission, did not really understand women. Why would he think that a bloody, smelly scalp would sway his wife in his favor? This we don't know, but we do know that the tactic didn't work. Lulu gave the scalp to a local department store, which maintained a small museum. Where it went from there we don't know.

When the Army put in its heavy guns—Crook, Terry, Miles—Cody was for a little while head of scouts. Even the luxury-loving Cody was a little put off by the luxury of Terry's command. The heavy guns saw very few Indians—only Mackenzie scored big. After a few months of pointless scouting Cody went downriver and resumed his acting career. It was mainly at Mackenzie's raid that the Sioux and Cheyenne encountered the enemy that John Wayne spoke about in John Ford's *The Searchers*: the whites who just kept coming, who fought in winter or the dead of night if the occasion demanded it.

After Mackenzie's raid, which occurred in November, the Indians may have known, subconsciously at least, that the whites were not going to back off: they were not going to stop until all the Indians were dead or reservationed, which was something next door to death for Indians who had always been free.

The real endgame for the plains Indians occurred in 1877. Red Cloud had long since stopped acting like a warrior and turned his skills to diplomacy. Negotiation was about all the Indians had left. Who would be sent where; which band would get the best places—this guaranteed little: if the land was really good it would soon be taken by the whites no matter what the treaties said. Mostly what the Indian leaders did was bargain for decent agents and regular rations.

No one liked Red Cloud much—no one on either side—but he had been negotiating for many years, and he understood the process better than many of the whites he worked with.

Crazy Horse, whose fame was rising, came in, in May of 1877. Some argue that Crazy Horse got north of Custer, at the Little Bighorn, and blocked his last possible route to escape—but this is arm-

RED CLOUD.

chair quarterbacking and cannot be proven either way. Like Custer's smile it is a hardy perennial of Little Bighorn gossip. They were on the same battlefield at least once, but no one can say with certainty that the two men ever glimpsed one another.

The best source for the smile is the diary of Private Thomas Coleman, the first American soldier to walk on the battlefield. It is a very well known account and I'll save it for when I end this book.

The common belief is that Custer smiled in the face of death, but in fact he may have died without knowing exactly what he faced. The smile could have been a rictus; some time passed before Private Coleman made his inspection.

Like so much about the Little Bighorn the smile is part of the vast amount of accumulated gossip. It's like the Matter of Troy, or some other national narrative cycle. We may speculate as much as we like, but we will never know.

Sitting Bull and Buffalo Bill.

BUFFALO BILL AND HIS HORSE.

BUFFALO BILL WITH RED CLOUD
AND AMERICAN HORSE.

BUFFALO BILL REENACTMENT OF INDIAN WARS.

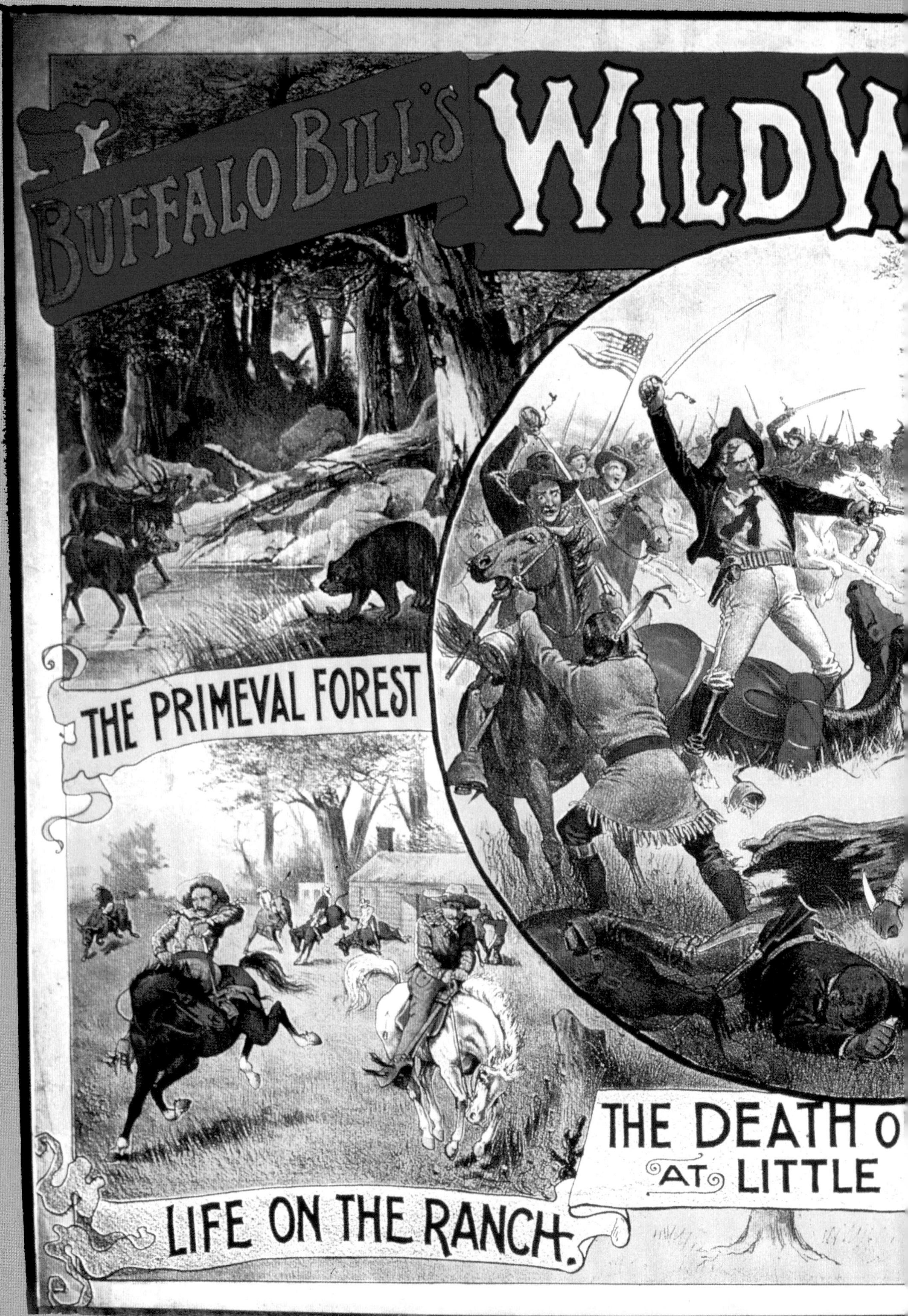

BUFFALO BILL'S WILD W

THE PRIMEVAL FOREST

THE DEATH O
AT LITTLE

LIFE ON THE RANCH.

EST IN THE MADISON·SQUARE· ·GARDEN·

THE CYCLONE IN THE MINING CAMP·

USTER
G HORN.

THE PRAIRIE FIRE.

COL.W.F.CODY

I AM COMING

Buffalo Bill promotional poster.

LIBBIE CUSTER WAS ASLEEP IN Fort Abraham Lincoln when definitive news of the massacre reached the fort. She may have shrieked once when she heard the news, but then she pulled herself together and pointed out to her handlers that she was an army wife and knew how to do these things. She was incensed to learn that the army was so sure she would become hysterical that they sent three men to wrestle her down. After all, she was the wife of the commander of the expedition; she had a duty to do.

And it was her job to accompany the death patrol around the fort and inform the other wives that they were now widows. The night was both cold and rainy, but, shivering, Libbie Custer did her duty.

Once the news spread around the world, Libbie had a longer, more difficult job to do: to defend Armstrong's reputation against the many critics who thought he was an unprincipled glory hound who had rashly caused the death of some 264 men, at least.

This long task—facing down hundreds of skeptics—must have been difficult. I have read her three books, all quite readable still, if finally shallow. If she was as cold as Benteen—or even occasionally Custer—suggest, then the books are really position papers and she stuck to them through the years. In the books she doesn't come across as cold; we have little evidence one way or another.

Her main tactic, though—making Marcus Reno the villain of the Little Bighorn—didn't work. Reno was not a very likable or particularly impressive officer, but he was not a total incompetent, either. At the Little Bighorn he did his fair best against odds that would have daunted many an officer. If he been a more likable man he would have had multitudes on his side.

Though his lack of likability was a defect, he *did* get acquitted; witness after witness testified that he had done the best he could against huge odds: if he had gone even a quarter of a mile farther he would have been annihilated, along with all his men.

Libbie Custer's half century of unwavering attacks on Major Marcus Reno hurt her worse than it hurt him. She became a shrill, obsessed woman, at least in the eyes of the military men who knew something about the battle. She thought Reno was a coward, while the Indians thought all the white soldiers were cowards—many, indeed, were cut down as they fled, a contemptible thing in Indian eyes. They killed the American cavalrymen so easily; they had expected far more opposition.

On his final expedition Custer wrote letters constantly—Libbie mentions one of forty-two pages, and, in fact, quite a few reached forty pages. Custer wrote fluently and he liked to write his wife, who was invited to many memorials and actually went to quite a few, but when someone in the War Department proposed putting up a statue of Major Reno, Libbie revolted big-time. Why honor the one coward in the battle? she wanted to know. Her very public claim that Reno was a coward was countered just as publicly by several military men, but Libbie doggedly made the same response: if Reno had fought harder her husband would still be alive.

Libbie's three books are *Boots and Saddles*, *Tenting on the Plains*, and *Following the Guidon*, the last named being by some measure the best. Libbie Custer had slowly but surely learned to write, and there is no trace in these books of the coldness Benteen complains of, though it's possible she was colder with her husband than with the people she ran into.

At the time of Custer's death she was thirty-five, and a very attractive woman. Despite a kind of dude ranch tone, her books are engaging. Libbie always casts herself as the dude, whether she's in Kansas, the Dakotas, or Texas.

There is a volume of the Custers' letters, edited in the 1940s by Marguerite Merrington, one of Libbie's friends. She is quite unable to cope with the many forty-pagers and seems to me to cut too much. Fashions in frankness changed about this

LIBBIE CUSTER, CIRCA *1895.*

time. Miss Merrington trimmed much that would be perfectly acceptable as epistles between husband and wife.

Custer had many terms of endearment: my little sunbeam, my little rosebud: not, perhaps, very original, but no doubt happily received in the bleakness of a Dakota military post.

34

THE EVER MATURING WORLD PRESS was ready for Custer, just as they were ready for the minor New Mexican outlaw known to the world as Billy the Kid.

All the papers wanted to know where, when, and how George Armstrong Custer died.

Soon the famous brewers of St. Louis chipped in with the *Last Stand* painting—and, perhaps just as important in spreading the dead Custer's fame, Buffalo Bill Cody, though no pal of Custer's, made "Custer's Last Stand" the finale of his Wild West Show, which toured very widely both in America and Western Europe.

Ironically, several of the Indians pretty much playing themselves in the Wild West

Show had indeed *been* themselves at the Little Bighorn itself. Among these were Sitting Bull—in the show but not the battle, and Black Elk, who became the Oglala sage.

Cody always firmly believed that he was showing history, not make-believe. Black Elk was about thirteen when the battle was fought—he is said to have taken a difficult scalp, a man with very short hair, hard to get ahold of.

To present to a civilized audience some of the actual Indians who had helped kill Custer, amounting to a very early reenactment, the Indians themselves did not seem to find it particularly odd.

The battle they flinched at reenacting was not the Little Bighorn, it was Wounded Knee. Yet Bill Cody was foolish enough to try and make a movie of Wounded Knee. It was called *The Indian Wars*; the Indians were afraid to act in it, thinking it might just be a new way to kill them. And when Cody brought Miles and other generals in as extras they feared even more.

Black Elk, famously, delivered the greatest elegy to Wounded Knee:

> I did not know then how much was ended. When I look back now from the hill of my old age I can still see the butchered women and children, lying heaped and scattered along one or another gulch as plain as when I was there with eyes still young. And I can say that something else died here in the bloody mud and was buried here in the blizzard. A people's dream died there. It had been a beautiful dream . . . now the nation's hoop is broken and scattered . . . there is no center anymore and the sacred tree is dead.

Many fine speeches by Native Americans echo Black Elk. The best of these can be found in a book edited by Peter Nabokov.

The aching need to have their own culture never left these people. Geronimo, reservationed at Fort Sill with Quanah Parker, never stopped beseeching the officials to let him go back to Arizona, where he would not last an hour because so many Arizonans hated him for the killing he had done. Yet still the old man wanted to go home.

The Indian victory at the Little Bighorn was not unique of its kind and in its time:

BLACK ELK.

Black Elk

in South Africa the Zulus overwhelmed the British garrison at Islanwanda and wiped them out to a man, and the Mahdi's forces did the same thing to General Gordon at Khartoum. In both cases, as with Custer, overwhelming numbers beat technological superiority.

But the two British defeats, *unlike* Custer's, were immediately and crushingly avenged. Kitchener decimated the Mahdi's forces; a fine account of his victory can be read in Winston Churchill's *The River War* (Churchill was there).

The poet Marianne Moore famously said that a poem should not mean, but be. What about battles. What did Waterloo really mean? or the Marne, or Stalingrad, El Alamein, Omaha Beach, and so on. Tolstoy worries the question of historical meaning in the infamous final section of *War and Peace*, proving very little and disappointing thousands upon thousands of readers.

The meaning, if any, of great battles is mainly to be found in shifts in political culture. Napoleon and after him Hitler didn't quite get to dominate the world, though narrow were the defeats.

The Little Bighorn, as I've said more than once already, was really the beginning of the end for Native American culture, while at least allowing them one last surge of native pride. Long Hair casually underestimated them, and, by golly, they showed him.

In the small town of Oberammergau, Germany, a famous Passion Play is performed every ten years. Custer's defeat and death at the Little Bighorn, which is reenacted every year, might be understood as an American Passion Play. Buffalo Bill Cody, great showman that he was, probably knew about the German Passion Play; he was also smart enough to know that the terrible clash by the little prairie river was an event that would be endlessly replayed—and now, nearly 140 years later, it *is* endlessly repeated.

Dramatically speaking, one of the things it had going for it was a powerful cast of characters. Performing for the American military were Custer, Mackenzie, Crook, Sherman, Sheridan, Miles, and Grant. For the natives we have Crazy Horse, Sitting Bull, Gall, Red Cloud, Dull Knife, Little Wolf, Spotted Tail, and others. It was always obvious who, in the long run, was going to win, making the gallantry of the losers even more appealing.

The play may actually have profited from having an unworthy hero: Custer, for all his early brilliance, was no Lee, Grant, Patton, Eisenhower. If he makes it into the top twenty American generals it is because of the fame he gained in defeat. He had sought this final battle without really knowing what he was doing. His military training deserted him and he caused the death of over 260 men.

Why, with so many marks against him, did he become an almost instant hero?

I think it was because the mechanisms were then fully in place. There was the press, and, importantly, there was the telegraph: the singing wires, as the Indians called it. For the first time in human history people could get the news when it was fresh. Journalism immediately flourished, aided by this new tool. Journalism exploded; the headline was invented, fanning the flames of patriotism: how dare the Indians kill our Custer, never mind that it had been his fault. The press had a field day with Custer and, in a sense, is still having it.

Then came the *camera*. Finally we could actually see what our leaders looked like, and, often, our enemies as well. Cameras went, in only a few years, to being in everyone's price range. They flooded the West as early as the 1840s, allowing people to see what previously they had only imagined. The only major Indian who eluded the camera was Crazy Horse, who refused to allow even the doctor who saved his wife's life to photograph him. But the others were not so quick. We can see Sitting Bull's hatred and Red Cloud's weariness. Custer and Libbie were both photographed often. Like the pictures of politicians or sports heroes the pictures bred a kind of false intimacy.

We rarely hear the names of these early Western photographers now, though they were quite important: Carleton Watkins, William Henry Jackson, and Timothy O'Sullivan captured much that otherwise would have been lost. I have thirty-seven glass negatives made by a woman photographer from Henrietta, Texas. They were made at Fort Sill and include unrecorded pictures of both Geronimo and Quanah Parker.

The Western photographers also managed to put the people in scale with the landscapes, to the amazement of Easterners.

The process of celebrity making worked quickly in Custer's case: all that was needed was for him to become posthumous. A big aid was the moving picture camera, which also got to the West quite early. Annie Oakley did a screen test for Mr. Edison in 1885, though vast, worldwide celebrity, of the sort enjoyed by Charlie Chaplin, probably didn't happen until the moving picture camera was in common use.

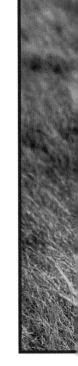

35

In my visits to the Custer battlefield, I found myself wondering why my fellow tourists were there. Few of them looked like history buffs. The battlefield was a major listing in the tour guides: it was just something you did if you were in that part of Montana. Great battlefields—the Marne, Omaha Beach, Stalingrad, Shiloh, Vicksburg, the Little Bighorn—are places where death once ruled, and people want to see what death left us: rows of crosses, mostly.

MONUMENT TO WHERE CUSTER FELL.

CUSTER'S TOMBSTONE.

MONUMENT TO THE 7TH CAVALRY.

We will never know what George Armstrong Custer felt when he waved to his troops and rode down that slope to meet his death. What he saw, in the short time he had to see anything, was an immense melee of horses and combatants. My guess is that the immense dust cloud so obscured the scene, or limited his focus, that he never really knew the extent of his own misjudgment. It may be that he even thought he was winning, until he was suddenly dead.

There is no more touching comment on the slaughter at the Little Bighorn than that made by Private Thomas Coleman, the first American soldier to walk the great deathscape by the little prairie river:

> Comes the most heartrending tale of all, as I have said before General
> Custer with five companies went below the Valley to cut them off as
> he Supposed but instead he was surrounded and all of them killed to a

man 14 officers and 350 Men Their bravest General of Modern times met his death with his two brothers, brother in law and nephew not 5 yards apart. Surrounded by 42 men of E Company. Oh what a slaughter how many homes made desolate by the Sad disaster everyone them was scalped and otherwise Mutiliated by the General he lay with a smile on his face.

ILLUSTRATION CREDITS

Adoe-photos/Art Resource, NY: p. 155.

The Art Archive at Art Resource, NY: p. 105.

© Bettmann/Corbis: pp. x, 60–61, 110–11, 124–25, 137, 156 top, 162.

Buffalo Bill Historical Center/The Art Archive at Art Resource, NY: title page, pp. 55, 61 top, 68–69, 120–21, 122–23, 126–27, 166.

Buyenlarge/Archive Photos/Getty Images, pp. 53, 74 left.

© Connie Ricca/Corbis: p. 171 left.

© Corbis: pp. 8 bottom, 28–29, 33, 34, 35 top, 36 top, 49, 50, 58 top, 59, 82–83, 89, 91 middle, 92 bottom, 100, 136 top, 138 top & bottom, 144 top & bottom, 157.

Custer Battlefield Museum: pp. 23, 30–31, 35 bottom, 82, 88.

David Francis Barry, Negative PORT 65 A 2, National Anthropological Archives, Smithsonian Institution: p. 106.

Denver Public Library, Western History Collection / The Bridgeman Art Library: pp. 3, 25, 32, 48 right, 70, 108, 133, 136 bottom, 153, 156 bottom.

Ellis County News, Hayes, KS: p. 20.

JFB / The Art Archive at Art Resource, NY: pp. 118–19.

Kean Collection/Archive Photos/Getty Images, pp. 66, 91 top.

Courtesy of © Heritage Auctions: 2

© Heritage Images/Corbis: p. 18.

Hulton Archive/Getty Images, p. 143.

© Hulton-Deutsch Collection/Corbis: pp. 12–13.

J.C. Custer Family Collection: p. 78 main picture and inset.

Library of Congress, Prints & Photographs Division, LC-USZ62–42305: p. 85; LC-DIG-stereo-1s00439: p. 142.

Little Bighorn Battlefield National Monument: pp. 35 middle, 62, 141.

© Marilyn Angel Wynn/Nativestock Pictures/Corbis: p. 87.

Matthew Brady: The Art Archive at Art Resource, NY: p. 6; Medford Historical Society Collection/Corbis: p. 24.

© Minnesota Historical Society/Corbis: p. 91 bottom.

Courtesy of The Monroe County Historical Museum: p. 146.

MPI/Archive Photos/Getty Images, pp. 40–41, 44, 65, 96, 139, 116–17.

National Geographic Image Collection/The Bridgeman Art Library: pp. 112–13.

National Portrait Gallery, Smithsonian Institution/Art Resource, NY: pp. 26, 45.

NGS Image Collection/The Art Archive at Art Resource, NY: p. 172.

Peter Newark Western Americana/The Bridgeman Art Library: p. 171 right.

PhotoQuest/Archive Photos/Getty Images, p. 46.

Private Collection/The Bridgeman Art Library: pp. 160–61.

Private Collection/Peter Newark Pictures/The Bridgeman Art Library: pp. 4, 10–11, 36 bottom, 48 left, 61 bottom, 74 right, 134, 151, 152, 158–59.

Private Collection/©Look and Learn/The Bridgeman Art Library: pp. 128–29.

Private Collection/Peter Newark Western Americana/The Bridgeman Art Library: p. 164.

Private Collection/Photo ©Tarker/The Bridgeman Art Library: p. 15.

Private Collection/The Stapleton Collection/The Bridgeman Art Library: endpapers, pp. 38, 140 top and bottom.

Randy Wells/Stone/Getty Images, pp. 174–75.

Smithsonian American Art Museum, Washington, DC/Art Resource, NY: pp. 8 top, 57, 58 bottom.

© Smithsonian Institution/Corbis: p. 147.

© Stapleton Collection/Corbis: pp. 114–15.

© Stephen G. Smith/Corbis: pp. 102–3.

Stock Sales WGBH/Scala/Art Resource, NY: p. 5.

Stock Montage/Archive Photos/Getty Images: p. 19.

© Swim Ink 2, LLC/Corbis: p. 1.

Time & Life Pictures/Getty Images: p. 92 top.

Transcendental Graphics/Archive Photos/Getty Images: p. 168.

Universal Images Group/Getty Images: p. 79.

West Point Museum Collection, United States Military Academy, West Point, New York: pp. 80–81, 98.

BIBLIOGRAPHY

Bourke, John. *Mackenzie's Last Fight with the Cheyenne.* New York, 1966.

Brown, Dee. *Bury My Heart at Wounded Knee.* New York, 1971.

Connell, Evan. *Son of the Morning Star.* San Francisco, 1984.

Custer, Elizabeth Bacon. *Boots and Saddles.* New York, 1985.

———. *Following the Guidon.* New York, 1893.

———. *Tenting on the Plains.* New York, 1890.

Custer, George Armstrong. *My Life on the Plains.* New York, 1995.

Donovan, James. *A Terrible Glory.* New York, 2008.

Elliott, Michael. *Custerology.* Chicago, 2007.

Leckie, Shirley A. *Elizabeth Baker Custer and the Making of a Myth.* Norman, 1993.

Nabokov, Peter, ed. *Native American Testimony.* New York, 1991.

Philbrick, Nathaniel. *The Last Stand.* New York, 2010.

Slotkin, Richard. *The Fatal Environment.* New York, 1985.

Utley, Robert. *Cavalier in Buckskin.* Norman, 1988.

———. *The Lance and the Shield.* New York, 1993.

There is, as I've said earlier, a vast literature, or subliterature, about Custer, most of it peculiar and most of it cranky. It reminds me somehow of the equally vast and cranky literature about Sherlock Holmes.

The literature the various Western groups publish is often to be found in "Brand Books," and other homemade amalgams, and addresses itself to every possible topic.